EGYPTIAN MAGIC

Spells, charms and rituals of ancient Egypt

EGYPTIAN MAGIC

Spells, charms and rituals of ancient Egypt

E. A. Wallis Budge

Disclaimer

Throughout the text readers may find that some of the language used and sentiments expressed are unacceptable by today's standards. These reflect the attitudes and usage common at the time the book was written. In no way do they reflect the attitude of the publishers.

PREFACE

A STUDY of the remains of the native religious literature of ancient Egypt which have come down to us has revealed the fact that the belief in magic, that is to say, in the power of magical names, and spells, and enchantments, and formulae, and pictures, and figures, and amulets, and in the performance of ceremonies accompanied by the utterance of words of power, to produce supernatural results, formed a large and important part of the Egyptian religion. And it is certain that, notwithstanding the continuous progress which the Egyptians made in civilization, and the high intellectual development to which they eventually attained, this belief influenced their minds and, from the earliest to the latest period of their history, shaped their views concerning things temporal as well as spiritual in a manner which, at this stage in the history of the world, is very difficult to understand. The scrupulous care with which they performed their innumerable religious ceremonies, and carried out the rules which they had formulated concerning the worship of the divine Power or powers, and their devotion to religious magic, gained for them among the nations with whom they came in contact the reputation of being at once the most religious and the most superstitious of men. That this reputation was, on the whole, well deserved, is the object of this little book to shew.

Egyptian magic dates from the time when the predynastic and prehistoric dwellers in Egypt believed that the earth, and the underworld, and the air, and the sky were peopled with countless beings, visible and invisible, which were held to be friendly or unfriendly to man according as the operations of nature, which they were supposed to direct, were favourable or unfavourable to him. In nature and attributes these beings were thought by primitive man to closely resemble himself and to possess all human passions, and emotions, and weaknesses, and defects; and the chief object of magic was to give man the pre-eminence over such beings. The favour of the beings who were placable and friendly to man might be obtained by means of gifts and offerings, but the cessation of hostilities on the part of those that were implacable and unfriendly could only be obtained by wheedling, and cajolery, and flattery, or by making use of an amulet, or secret name, or magical formula, or figure, or picture which had the effect of bringing to the aid of the mortal who possessed it the power of a being that was mightier than the foe who threatened to do evil to him. The magic of most early nations aimed at causing the transference of power from a supernatural being to man, whereby he was to be enabled to obtain superhuman results and to become for a time as mighty as the original possessor of the power; but the object of Egyptian magic was to endow man with the means of compelling both friendly and hostile powers, nay, at a later time, even God Himself, to do what he wished, whether the were willing or not. The belief in magic, the word being used in its best sense, is older in Egypt than the belief in God, and it is certain that a very large number of the Egyptian religious ceremonies, which were performed in later times as an integral part of a highly spiritual worship, had their origin in superstitious customs which date from a period when God, under any name or in any form, was unconceived in the minds of the Egyptians. Indeed it is probable that even the use of the sign which represents an axe, and which stands the hieroglyphic character both for God and "god," indicates that this weapon and tool was employed in the performance of some ceremony connected with religious magic in prehistoric, or at any rate in predynastic times, when it in some mysterious way symbolized the presence of a supreme Power. But be this as it may, it is quite certain that magic and religion developed and flourished side by side in Egypt throughout all periods of her history, and that any investigation which we may make of the one necessarily includes an examination of the other.

From the religious books of ancient Egypt we learn that the power possessed by a priest or man who was skilled in the knowledge and working of magic was believed to be almost boundless. By pronouncing certain words or names of power in the proper manner and in the proper tone of voice he could heal the sick, and cast out the evil spirits which caused pain and suffering in those who were diseased, and restore the dead to life, and bestow upon the dead man the power to transform the corruptible into an incorruptible body, wherein the soul might live to all eternity. His words enabled human beings to assume divers forms at will, and to project their souls into animals and other creatures; and in obedience to his commands, inanimate figures and pictures became living beings and things which hastened to perform his behests. The powers of nature acknowledged his might, and wind and rain, storm and tempest, river and sea, and disease and death worked evil and ruin upon his foes, and upon the enemies of those who were provided with the knowledge of the words which he had wrested from the gods of heaven, and earth, and the underworld.

Inanimate nature likewise obeyed such words of power, and even the world itself came into existence through the utterance of a word by Thoth; by their means the earth could be rent asunder, and the waters forsaking their nature could be piled up in a heap, and even the sun's course in the heavens could be stayed by a word. No god, or spirit, or devil, or fiend, could resist words of power, and the Egyptians invoked their aid in the smallest as well as in the greatest events of their lives. To him that was versed in the lore contained in the books of the "double house of life" the future was as well known as the past, and neither time nor distance could limit the operations of his power; the mysteries of life and death were laid bare before him, and he could draw aside the veil which hid the secrets of fate and destiny from the knowledge of ordinary mortals.

Now if views such as these concerning the magician's power were held by the educated folk of ancient Egypt there is little to wonder at when we find that beliefs and superstitions of the most degraded character flourished with rank luxuriance among the peasants and working classes of that country, who failed to understand the symbolism of the elaborate ceremonies which were performed in the temples, and who were too ignorant to distinguish the spiritual conceptions which lay at their root – to meet the religious needs of such people the magician, and in later times the priest, found it necessary to provide pageants and ceremonies which appealed chiefly to the senses, and following their example, unscrupulous but clever men took advantage of the ignorance of the general public and pretended to knowledge of the supernatural, and laid claim to the possession of power over gods, and spirits, and demons. Such false knowledge and power they sold for money, and for purposes of gain the so-called magician was ready to further any sordid transaction or wicked scheme which his dupe wished to carry out. This magic degenerated into sorcery, and demonology, and wit craft, and those who dealt in it were regarded as associates of the Devil, and servants of the powers of darkness, and workers of the "black art." In the "white" and "black" magic of the Egyptians most of the magic known in the other countries of the world may be found; it is impossible yet to say exactly how much the beliefs and religious systems of other nations were influenced by them, but there is no doubt that certain views and religious ideas of many heathen and Christian sects may be traced directly to them. Many interesting proofs might be adduced in support of this statement, but the limits of this book will not admit of their being given here.

When we consider the lofty spiritual character of the greater part of the Egyptian religion, and remember its great antiquity, it is hard to understand why the Egyptians carefully preserved in their writings and ceremonies so much which savoured of gross and childish superstition, and which must have been the product of their predynastic or prehistoric ancestors, even during the period of their greatest intellectual enlightenment. But the fact remains that they did believe in One God Who was almighty, and eternal, and invisible, Who created the heavens, and the earth, and all beings and things therein; and in the resurrection of the body in a changed and glorified form, which would live to all eternity in the company of the spirits and souls of the righteous in a kingdom ruled by a being who was of divine origin, but who had lived upon the earth, and had suffered a cruel death at the hands of his enemies, and had risen from the dead, and had become the God and king of the world which is beyond the grave; and that, although they believed all these things and proclaimed their belief with almost passionate earnestness, they seem never to have freed themselves from a hankering after amulets and talismans, and magical names, and words of power, and seem to have trusted in these to save their souls and bodies, both living and dead, with something of the same confidence which they placed in the death and resurrection of Osiris. A matter for surprise is that they seem to see nothing incongruous in such a mixture of magic and religion, and the general attitude of the mind of the Egyptian on the point is well illustrated by the following facts. Attached to the service of Râ, the Sun-god, at Thebes were numerous companies of priests whose duties consisted as much in making copies of religious books and in keeping alive the "divine traditions," as in ministering to the god in their appointed seasons. The members of these companies who wrote the copies of the Book of the Dead which were buried with kings and queens and personages of royal or exalted rank declared the power and omnipotence of Almighty God, Whose visible emblem to mankind was the Sun, and His sovereignty over things celestial and things terrestrial with no uncertain voice, and we should expect them to believe what they proclaimed, *i.e.* that God was sufficiently powerful to protect His emblem in the sky. Yet the priests of Thebes made copies of works which contained texts to be recited at specified hours of the day and night, and gave directions for the performance of magical ceremonies, the avowed object of such being to prevent the mythical monster Âpep from vanquishing the Sun-god. And it is stated in all seriousness that if a piece of papyrus upon which a figure of the monster has been drawn, and a wax figure of him be burnt in a fire made of a certain kind of grass, and the prescribed words be recited over them as they burn, the Sun-god will be delivered from Âpep, and that neither rain, nor cloud, nor mist shall be able to prevent his light from falling upon the earth. Moreover, the rubric describes the performance of the ceremony as a meritorious act!

E. A. WALLIS BUDGE.

LONDON,

August 28th, 1899

CONTENTS

INTRODUCTION

E.A. Wallis Budge (1857-1934) was a prominent British Egyptologist, renowned for his extensive work on ancient Egyptian history, language and culture. Born in Bodmin, Cornwall, Budge developed an early interest in languages and antiquities, which led him to pursue studies at Cambridge University.

Budge's career took a significant turn when he joined the British Museum in 1883, initially working as an assistant in the Department of Egyptian and Assyrian Antiquities. His remarkable talent and dedication soon earned him the position of Keeper of the Department, a role he held from 1894 until his retirement in 1924. During his tenure, Budge conducted numerous expeditions to Egypt and Sudan, acquiring a vast collection of artifacts and manuscripts for the British Museum. His efforts significantly enriched the museum's holdings and contributed to the broader understanding of Egyptian civilization. However, he was also instrumental in bringing information about ancient Egypt to the general reader.

Budge's scholarly output was prolific, with over 140 books and articles to his name. Among his most notable works are *The Book of the Dead*, *Egyptian Magic* and *The Gods of the Egyptians*, which remain influential in the field of Egyptology. He was particularly adept at translating ancient texts, making these works accessible for the first time to both scholars and the general public.

Despite his contributions, Budge's methods and interpretations have faced criticism. Some contemporaries and modern scholars argue that his acquisition practices were ethically questionable and that his translations lacked accuracy due to his tendency to prioritize narrative appeal over strict scholarly rigour.

Nonetheless, Budge's legacy endures through his extensive contributions to Egyptology and the popularization of ancient Egyptian culture. His work laid foundational stones for future research and continues to inspire both academic and public interest in one of the world's oldest and most fascinating civilizations.

CHAPTER I

ANTIQUITY OF MAGICAL PRACTICES IN EGYPT

IN the first volume of this series an attempt was made to set before the reader a statement of the ideas and beliefs which the ancient Egyptians held in respect of God, the "gods," the Judgment, the Resurrection, and Immortality; in short, to sketch in brief outline much of what was beautiful, and noble, and sublime in their religion. The facts of this statement were derived wholly from native religious works, the latest of which is some thousands of years old, and the earliest of which may be said to possess an antiquity of between six and seven thousand years; the extracts quoted in support of the deductions set forth in it were intended to enable the reader to judge for himself as to the general accuracy of the conclusions there given. Many writers on the Egyptian religion have somewhat blinked the fact that it had two sides; on the one it closely resembles in many respects the Christian religion of to-day, and on the other the religion of many of the sects which flourished in the first three or four centuries of our era, and which may be said to have held beliefs which were part Christian and part non-Christian. In its non-Christian aspect it represents a collection of ideas and superstitions which belong to a savage or semi-savage state of existence, and which maintained their hold in a degree upon the minds of the Egyptians long after they had advanced to a high state of civilization. We may think that such ideas and beliefs are both childish and foolish, but there is no possible reason for doubting that they were very real things to those who held them, and whether they are childish or foolish or both they certainly passed into the religion of the people of Egypt, wherein they grew and flourished, and were, at least many of them, adopted by the Egyptian converts to Christianity, or Copts. Reference is made to them in the best classical works of the ancient Egyptians, and it is more than probable that from them they found their way into the literatures of the other great nations of antiquity, and through the Greeks, Romans, Arabs, and others into the countries of Europe. In the following pages an attempt will be made to place in the reader's hands the evidence as to the magical side of the Egyptian religion, which would have been out of place in the former work, the object of which was to describe beliefs of a more spiritual nature. But, as in the book on the Egyptian Ideas of the Future Life, the facts here given are drawn from papyri and other native documents, and the extracts are quoted from compositions which were actually employed by the Egyptians to produce magical effects.

The "magic" of the Egyptians was of two kinds: (1) that which was employed for legitimate purposes and with the idea of benefiting either the living or the dead, and (2) that which was made use of in the furtherance of nefarious plots and schemes and was intended to bring calamities upon those against whom it was directed. In the religious texts and works we see how magic is made to be the handmaiden of religion, and how it appears in certain passages side by side with the most exalted spiritual conceptions; and there can be no doubt that the chief object of magical books and ceremonies was to benefit those who had by some means attained sufficient knowledge to make use of them. But the Egyptians were unfortunate enough not to be understood by many of the strangers who found their way into their country, and as a result wrong and exaggerated ideas of their religion were circulated among the surrounding nations, and the magical ceremonies which were performed at their funerals were represented by the ignorant either as silly acts of superstition or as tricks of the "black" art. But whereas the magic of every other nation of the ancient East was directed entirely against the powers of darkness, and was invented in order to frustrate their fell designs by invoking a class of benevolent beings to their aid, the Egyptians aimed being able to command their gods to work for them, and to compel them to appear at their desire. These great results were to be obtained by the use of certain words which, to be efficacious, must be uttered in a proper tone of voice by a duly qualified man; such words might be written upon some substance, papyrus, precious stones, and the like, and worn on the person, when their effect could be transmitted to any distance. As almost every man, woman, and child in Egypt who could afford it wore some such charm or talisman, it is not to be wondered at that the Egyptians were at a very early period regarded as a nation of magicians and sorcerers. Hebrew, and Greek, and Roman writers referred to them as experts in the occult sciences, and as the possessors of powers which could, according to circumstances, be employed to do either good or harm to man.

From the Hebrews we receive, incidentally, it is true, considerable information about the powers of the Egyptian magician. Saint Stephen boasts that the great legislator Moses "was learned in all the wisdom of the Egyptians," and declares that he "was mighty in words and in deeds," and there are numerous features in the life of this remarkable man which shew that he was acquainted with many of the practices of Egyptian magic. The phrase "mighty in words" probably means that, like the goddess Isis, he was "strong of tongue" and uttered the words of power which he knew with correct pronunciation, and halted not in his speech, and was perfect both in giving the command and in saying the word. The turning of a serpent into what is apparently an inanimate, wooden stick, and the turning of the stick back into a writhing snake, are feats which have been performed in the East from the most ancient period; and the power to control and direct the movements of such venomous reptiles was one of the things of which the Egyptian was most proud, and in which he was most skilful, already in the time when the pyramids were being built. But this was by no means the only proof which Moses gives that he was versed in the magic of the Egyptians, for, like the sage Âba-aner and king Nectanebus, and all the other magicians of Egypt from time immemorial, he and Aaron possessed a wonderful rod by means of which they worked their wonders. At the word of Moses Aaron lifted up his rod and smote the waters and they became blood; he stretched it out over the waters, and frogs innumerable appeared; when the dust was smitten by the rod it became lice; and so on. Moses sprinkled ashes "toward heaven," and it became boils and blains upon man and beast; he stretched out his rod, and there was "hail, and fire mingled with the hail, very grievous," and the "flax and the barley was smitten;" he stretched out his rod and the locusts came, and after them the darkness. Now Moses did all these things, and brought about the death of the firstborn among the Egyptians by the command of his God, and by means of the words which He told him to speak. But although we are told by the Hebrew writer that the Egyptian magicians could not imitate all the miracles of Moses, it is quite certain that every Egyptian magician believed that he could perform things equally marvellous by merely uttering the name of one of his gods, or through the words of power which he had learned to recite; and there are many instances on record of Egyptian magicians utterly destroying their enemies by the recital of a few words possessed of magical power, and, by the performance of some, apparently, simple ceremony. But one great distinction must be made between the magic of Moses and that of the Egyptians among whom he lived; the former was wrought by the command of the God of the Hebrews, but the latter by the gods of Egypt at the command of man.

Later on in the history of Moses' dealings with the Egyptians we find the account of how "he stretched out his hand over the sea, and the Lord caused the sea to go *back* by a strong east wind all that night, and made the sea dry *land*, and the waters were divided. And the children of Israel went into the midst of the sea upon the dry *ground*; and the waters *were* a wall unto them on their right hand, and on their left." When the Egyptians had come between the two walls of water, by God's command Moses stretched forth his hand over the sea, "and the sea returned to his strength," and the "waters returned, and covered the chariots, and the horsemen, *and* all the host of Pharaoh that came into the sea after them." But the command of the waters of the sea or river was claimed by the Egyptian magician long before the time of Moses, as we may see from an interesting story preserved in the Westcar Papyrus. This document was written in the early part of the XVIIIth dynasty, about B.C. 1550 but it is clear that the stories in it date from the Early Empire, and are in fact as old as the Great Pyramid. The story is related to king Khufu (Cheops) by Baiu-f-Râ as an event which happened in the time of the king's father, and as a proof of the wonderful powers of magic which were possessed by the priest called Tchatcha-em-ânkh. It seems that on a certain day king Seneferu was in low spirits, and he applied to the nobles of his royal household expecting that they would find some means whereby his heart might be made glad; but as they could do nothing to

25

cheer up the king, he gave orders that the priest and writer of books, Tchatcha-em-ânkh, should be brought into his presence immediately, and in accordance with the royal command he was at once brought. When he had arrived, Seneferu said to him, "My brother, I turned to the nobles of my royal household seeking for some means whereby I might cheer my heart, but they have found nothing for me." Then the priest made answer and advised the king to betake himself to the lake near the palace, and to go for a sail on it in a boat which had been comfortably furnished with things from the royal house. "For," said he, "the heart of thy Majesty will rejoice and be glad when thou sailest about hither and thither, and dost see the beautiful thickets which are on the lake, and when thou seest the pretty banks thereof and the beautiful fields then shall thy heart feel happiness." He next begged that the king would allow him to organize the journey, and asked his permission to let him bring twenty ebony paddles inlaid with gold, and also twenty young virgins having beautiful heads of hair and lovely forms and shapely limbs, and twenty nets wherein these virgins may array themselves instead of in their own ordinary garments. The virgins were to row and sing to his Majesty. To these proposals the king assented, and when all was ready he took his place in the boat; while the young women were rowing him about hither and thither the king watched them, and his heart became released from care. Now as one of the young women was rowing, she entangled herself in some way in her hair, and one of her ornaments which was made of "new turquoise" fell into the water and sank; she ceased to row, and not herself only, but all the other maidens ceased to row also. When the king saw that the maidens had ceased from their work, he said to them, "Will ye not row?" and they replied, "Our leader has ceased to row." Then turning to the maiden who had dropped her ornament overboard, he asked her why she was not rowing, whereupon she told him what had happened. On this the king promised that he would get back the ornament for her.

Then the king commanded that Tchatcha-em-ânkh should appear before him at once, and as soon as the sage had been brought into his presence he said to him, "O Tchatcha-em-ânkh, my brother, I have done according to thy words, and the heart of my Majesty became glad when I saw how the maidens rowed. But now, an ornament which is made of new turquoise and belongeth to one of the maidens who row hath fallen into the water, and she hath in consequence become silent, and hath ceased to row, and hath disturbed the rowing of those in her company. I said to her, 'Why dost thou not row?' and she replied, 'An ornament [of mine] made of new turquoise hath fallen into

the water.' Then I said to her, 'I will get it back for thee.'"
Thereupon the priest and writer of books Tchatcha-em-
ânkh spake certain words of power (*hekau*), and having
thus caused one section of the water of the lake to go up
upon the other, he found the ornament lying upon a pot-
sherd, and he took it and gave it to the maiden. Now the
water was twelve cubits deep, but when Tchatcha-em-ânkh
had lifted up one section of the water on to the other, that
portion became four and twenty cubits deep. The magician
again uttered certain words of power, and the water
of the lake became as it had been before he had caused
one portion of it to go up on to the other; and the king
prepared a feast for all his royal household, and rewarded
Tchatcha-em-ânkh with gifts of every kind. Such is a story
of the power possessed by a magician in the time of king
Khufu (Cheops), who reigned at the beginning of the IVth
dynasty, about B.C. 3800. The copy of the story which we
possess is older than the period when Moses lived, and thus
there can be no possibility of our seeing in it a distorted
version of the miracle of the waters of the sea standing like
walls, one on the right hand and one on the left; on the
other hand Moses' miracle may well have some connexion
with that of Tchatcha-em-ânkh.

Among the Greeks and Romans considerable respect
was entertained, not only for the "wisdom" of the

Egyptians, but also for the powers of working magic which they were supposed to possess. The Greek travellers who visited Egypt brought back to their own country much information concerning its religion and civilization, and, though they misunderstood many things which they saw and heard there, some of the greatest of thinkers among the Greeks regarded that country not only as the home of knowledge and the source of civilization and of the arts, but also as the fountain head of what has been called "white magic," and the "black art." In some respects they exaggerated the powers of the Egyptians, but frequently when the classical writers were well informed they only ascribed to them the magical knowledge which the Egyptian magicians themselves claimed to possess. A striking instance of this is given in the second book of the *Metamorphoses of Apuleius* where, it will be remembered, the following is narrated. The student Telephron arrived one day at Larissa, and as he was wandering about in an almost penniless condition he saw an old man standing on a large block of stone issuing a proclamation to the effect that any one who would undertake to guard a dead body should receive a good reward. When Telephron asked if dead men were in the habit of running away the old man replied testily to the effect that the witches all over Thessaly used to tear off pieces of flesh from the faces of the dead with their teeth, in order to make magical spells by means of them, and to prevent this dead bodies must needs be watched at night. The young man then asked what his duties would be if he undertook the post, and he was told that he would have to keep thoroughly awake all night, to gaze fixedly upon the dead body, to look neither to the right hand nor to the left, and not to close the eyes even to wink. This was absolutely necessary because the witches were able to get out of their skins and to take the form of a bird, or dog, or mouse, and their craftiness was such that they could take the forms of flies and cast sleep upon the watcher. If the watcher relaxed his attention and the body became mutilated by the witches, the pieces of flesh torn away would have to be made good from the body of the watcher Telephron agreed to undertake the duty for one thousand nummi, and was led by the old man to a house, and, having been taken into the room where the dead body was, found a man making notes on tablets to the effect that nose, eyes, ears, lips, chin, etc., were untouched and whole. Having been provided with a lamp and some oil that night he began his watch, and all went well, notwithstanding that he was greatly afraid, until the dead of night when a weasel came into the chamber and looked confidingly at the watcher; but he drove the animal – which was no doubt a witch – from the room, and then fell fast asleep. In the early morning he was suddenly wakened by the trumpets of the soldiers, and almost immediately the widow of the dead man came to him with seven witnesses, and began to examine the body to see if it was intact; finding that no injury had been done to it she ordered her steward to pay Telephron his fee, and was so grateful to him that she promised to make him one of her household. In attempting to express his thanks, however, he made use of some inauspicious words, and immediately the servants of the house fell upon him, and buffeted him, and plucked out his hair by the roots, and tore his clothes, and finally cast him out of the house. Soon afterwards, whilst wandering about, he saw the funeral procession pass through the forum, and at that moment an old man went to the bier, and with sobs and tears accused the widow of poisoning his nephew so that she might inherit his property and marry her lover. Presently the mob which had gathered together wanted to set her house on fire, and some people began to stone her; the small boys also threw stones at her. When she had denied the accusation, and had called upon the gods to be witnesses of her innocence, the old man cried out, "Let, then, Divine Providence decide the truth, in answer to her denial. Behold, the famous prophet Zaclas the Egyptian, dwelleth among us, and he hath promised me that for much money he will make the soul of the dead man to return from the place of death in the underworld, and to make it to dwell in his body again for a short time." With these words, he led forward a man dressed in linen, and wearing palm-leaf sandals, who, like all the Egyptian priests, had his head shaved, and having kissed his hands and embraced his legs he implored him by the stars, and by the gods of the underworld, and by the island of the Nile, and by the Inundation, etc., to restore life to the dead body, if only for the smallest possible time, so that the truth of his accusation against the widow might be proved. Thus adjured Zaclas touched the mouth and the breast of the dead man three times with some plant, and having turned his face to the East and prayed, the lungs of the corpse began to fill with breath, and his heart to beat, and raising his head and shoulders he asked why he had been called back to life, and then he begged to be allowed to rest in peace. At this moment Zaclas addressed him, and telling him that he had the power, through his prayers, to cause the fiends to come and torture him, ordered him to make known the means by which he had died. With a groan he replied that the wife whom he had recently married gave him poison to drink, and that he died in consequence. The wife at once contradicted the words of her husband, and of the people who were standing round some took one side and some another. At length the husband declared that he would prove the truth of his own words, and pointing to Telephron, who had attempted to guard his body, told those present that the witches after making many attempts to elude his vigilance had cast deep sleep upon him. They next called upon himself by his name, which happened to be Telephron, like that of his watcher, and whilst he was endeavouring feebly to obey their spells, his watcher rose up unconsciously and walked about. Seeing this the witches forced their way into the room through some unknown place, and having taken off the nose and ears of the watcher they placed models of these members in their places. Those who heard these words looked fixedly at the young man, who at once put up his hands and touched the members, whereupon his nose came off in his hand, and his cars slipped through his fingers on to the ground.

The end of the story does not concern us, and so we pass on to note that the act of touching the mouth which Zaclas performed is, of course, a part of the ceremony of "opening the mouth" which is so often referred to in religious texts, and was considered of extreme importance for the welfare of the dead, and that the power of bringing back the dead to life which Apuleius ascribes to the priest or magician was actually claimed some thousands of years before Christ by the sages of Egypt, as we may see from the following story in the Westcar Papyrus.

A son of king Khufu (or Cheops, who reigned about B.C. 3800) called Herutâtâf, who was famous as a learned man and whose name is preserved in the "Book of the Dead" in connection with the "discovery" of certain Chapters of that wonderful compilation, was one day talking to his father, presumably on the subject of the powers of working magic possessed by the ancients. In answer to some remark by Khufu he replied, "Up to the present thou hast only heard reports concerning the things which the men of olden time knew, and man knoweth not whether they are true or not; but now I will cause thy Majesty to see a sage in thine own time, and one who knoweth thee not." In reply to Khufu's question, "Who is this man, O Herutâtâf?" the young man replied, "It is a certain man called Teta, who dwelleth in Tet-Seneferu, and is one hundred and ten years old, and to this very day he eateth five hundred loaves of bread, and the shoulder of an ox, and he drinketh one hundred measures of ale. He knoweth how to fasten on again to its body a head that hath been cut off; he knoweth how to make a lion follow him whilst his snare is trailing on the ground; and he knoweth the number of the *aptet* of the sanctuary of Thoth." Now Khufu had for a long time past sought out the aptet of the sanctuary of Thoth, because he was anxious to make one similar for his own "horizon." Though at the present it is impossible to say what the *aptet* was, it is quite clear that it was an object or instrument used in connection with the working of magic of some sort, and it is clear that the king was as much interested in the pursuit as his subjects. In reply to his son's words Khufu told him to go and bring the sage into his presence, and the royal barge or boat having been brought, Herutâtâf set out for the place where the sage dwelt. Having sailed up the river some distance he and his party arrived at Tet-Seneferu, and when the boats had been tied to the quay the prince set out to perform the rest of the Journey, which was overland, in a sort of litter made of ebony, which was borne by men by means of poles of *sesnetchem* wood, inlaid with gold. When he had arrived at the abode of Teta, the litter was set down upon the ground, and the prince came out to greet the sage, whom he found lying upon a basket-work bed or mattress, which had been placed for him in the courtyard of his house, whilst one servant shampooed his head, and another rubbed his feet. After a suitable greeting and reference to the sage's honourable condition had been made, Herutâtâf told him that he had come from a great distance in order to bring to him a message from Khufu his father, and the sage bade him "Welcome" heartily, and prophesied that Khufu would greatly exalt his rank. The greetings ended, Herutâtâf assisted Teta to rise, and the old man set out for the quay leaning upon the arm of the king's son, and when he had arrived there he asked that a boat might be provided for the transport of his children and his books. Two boats were at once prepared and filled with their complement of sailors, and Teta sailed down the Nile with Herutâtâf, while his family followed.

After a time the party arrived at Khufu's palace, and Herutâtâf went into the presence of his father, and reported to him that he had brought Teta the sage for him to see; Khufu gave orders that he was to be brought before him quickly, and having gone forth into the colonnade of the palace, Teta was led in to him. Khufu said to him, "How is it, Teta, that I have never seen thee?" and the sage replied, "O Prince, he who is called cometh; and since thou hast called me, behold, here I am." Khufu said to him, "Is it true, according to what is reported, that thou knowest how to fasten on again to its body the head which hath been cut off?" and the sage replied, "Yea, verily, O my lord the Prince, I do know how to do this thing." And Khufu said, "Let a captive who is shut up in prison be brought to me so that I may inflict his doom upon him," but Teta made answer, "Nay, my lord the king let not this thing be performed upon man, but upon some creature that belongeth to the sacred animals." Then some one brought to him a goose, and having cut off its head, he laid the body of the goose on the west side of the colonnade, and the head on the east side. Teta then stood up and spake certain words of magical power, whereupon the body began to move and the head likewise, and each time that they moved the one came nearer to the other, until at length the head moved to its right place on the bird, which straightway cackled. After this Teta had a *khet-âa* bird brought to him, and upon it he performed the same miracle which he had wrought upon the goose; and to prove that he had similar power over the animal creation, an ox was brought to him, and having cut off its head, which fell upon the ground, he uttered words of magical power, and the ox stood up and lived as before.

The two stories from the Westcar Papyrus given above are sufficient to prove that already in the IVth dynasty the working of magic was a recognized art among the Egyptians, and everything we learn from later texts indicates that it is well-nigh impossible to imagine a time in Egypt when such was not the case. But the "wisdom" of the Egyptians was of two kinds, that is to say, they were possessed of the two kinds of "wisdom" which enabled them to deal with both the material world and the spiritual world; the nations around, however, confused the two kinds, and misunderstood matters in consequence.

One of the oldest names of Egypt is "Kamt" or "Qemt," a word which means "black" or "dusky," and it was applied to the country on account of the dark colour of the mud which forms the land on each side of the Nile; the Christian Egyptians or Copts transmitted the word under the form Khême to the Greeks, Romans, Syrians, and Arabs. At a very early period the Egyptians were famous for their skill in the working of metals and in their attempts to transmute them, and, according to Greek writers, they employed quicksilver in the processes whereby they separated the metals gold and silver from the native ore. From these processes there resulted a "black" powder or substance which was supposed to possess the most marvellous powers, and to contain in it the individualities of the various metals; and in it their actual substances were incorporated. In a mystical manner this "black" powder was identified with the body which the god Osiris was known to possess in the underworld, and to both were attributed magical qualities, and both were thought to be sources of life and power. Thus, side by side with the growth of skill in performing the ordinary processes of metal-working, in Egypt, there grew up in that country the belief that magical powers existed in fluxes and alloys; and the art of manipulating the metals, and the knowledge of the chemistry of the metals and of their magical powers were described by, the name "Khemeia." that is to say "the preparation of the black ore" (or "powder") which was regarded as the transmutation of metals. To this name the Arabs affixed the article *al*, and thus we obtain the word Al-Khemeia, or Alchemy, which will perpetuate the reputation of the Egyptians as successful students both of "white magic" and of the "black" art.

But in addition to their skill as handicraftsmen and artisans the Egyptians were skilled in literary composition, and in the production of books, especially of that class which related to the ceremonies which were performed for the benefit of the dead. We have, unfortunately, no means of knowing what early contemporary peoples thought of the Egyptian funeral ceremonies, but it seems to be certain that it was chiefly by means of these that they obtained their reputation as workers of miracles. If by chance any members of a desert tribe had been permitted to behold the ceremonies which were performed when the kings for whom the Pyramids had been built were laid to rest in them, the stories that they took back to their kinsmen would be received as sure proofs that the Egyptians had the power to give life to the dead, to animate statues, and to command the services of their gods by the mere utterance of their names as words of power. The columns of hieroglyphics with which the walls of the tombs were often covered, and the figures of the gods, painted or sculptured upon stelae or sarcophagi, would still further impress the barbarian folk who always regard the written letter and

39

those who understand it with great awe. The following story from Mas'ûdî will illustrate the views which the Arabs held concerning the inscriptions and figures of gods in the temples of Egypt. It seems that when the army of Pharaoh had been drowned in the Red Sea, the women and slaves feared lest they should be attacked by the kings of Syria and the West; in this difficulty they elected a woman called Dalûkah as their queen, because she was wise and prudent and skilled in magic. Dalûkah's first act was to surround all Egypt with a wall, which she guarded by men who were stationed along it at short intervals, her object being as much to protect her son, who was addicted to the chase, from the attacks of wild beasts as Egypt from invasion by nomad tribes; besides this she placed round the enclosure figures of crocodiles and other formidable animals. During the course of her reign of thirty years she filled Egypt with her temples and with figures of animals; she also made figures of men in the form of the dwellers in the countries round about Egypt, and in Syria, and in the West, and of the beasts which they rode. In the temples she collected all the secrets of nature and all the attracting or repelling powers which were contained in minerals, plants, and animals. She performed her sorceries at the moment in the revolution of the celestial bodies when they would be amenable to a higher power. And it came to pass that if an army set out from any part of Arabia or Syria to attack Egypt, the queen made the figures of its soldiers and of the animals which they were riding to disappear beneath the ground, and the same fate immediately overtook the living creatures which they represented, wherever they might be on their journey, and the destruction of the figures on sculptures entailed the destruction of the hostile host. In brief, the large figures of the gods which were sculptured or painted on the walls, and the hieroglyphic inscriptions which accompanied them, were considered by those who could neither understand nor read them to be nothing more nor less than magical figures and formulae which were intended to serve as talismans.

The historian Mas'ûdî mentions an instance of the powers of working magic possessed by a certain Jew, which proves that the magical practices of the Egyptians had passed eastwards and had found a congenial home among the Jews who lived in and about Babylon. This man was a native of the village of Zurârah in the district of Kûfa, and he employed his time in working magic. In the Mosque at Kûfa, and in the presence of Walîd ibn Ukbah, he raised up several apparitions, and made a king of huge stature, who was mounted upon a horse, gallop about in the courtyard of the Mosque. He then transformed himself into a camel and walked upon a rope; and made the phantom of an ass

41

to pass through his body; and finally having slain a man, he cut off the head and removed it from the trunk, and then by passing his sword over the two parts, they united and the man came alive again. This last act recalls the joining of the head of the dead goose to its body and the coming back of the bird to life which has been described above.

We have now to describe briefly the principal means upon which the Egyptians relied for working magic, that is to say, magical stones or amulets, magical figures, magical pictures and formulae, magical names, magical ceremonies, etc., and such portions of the Book of the Dead as bear upon these subjects generally.

CHAPTER II

MAGICAL STONES OR AMULETS

"AMULET" is a name given to a class of objects and ornaments, and articles of dress and wearing apparel, made of various substances which were employed by the Egyptians, and later by other nations, to protect the human body, either living or dead, from baleful influences, and from the attacks of visible and invisible foes. The word "amulet" is derived from an Arabic root meaning "to bear, to carry," hence "amulet" is "something which is carried or worn," and the name is applied broadly to any kind of talisman or ornament to which supernatural powers are ascribed. It is not clear whether the amulet was intended first of all to protect the living or the dead body, but it seems that it was originally worn to guard its owner from savage animals and from serpents. As time went on the development of religious ideas and beliefs progressed, and as a result new amulets representing new views were invented; and the objects which were able to protect the living were made, by an easy transition in the minds of those who wore them, to protect the dead. Moreover, as the preservation of the corruptible body, with the number of its members complete and intact, was of the most vital importance for the life of the spiritual and incorruptible body which was believed to spring therefrom, under the influence of the new beliefs the dead body became a veritable storehouse of amulets. Each member was placed under the specific protection of some amulet, and a number of objects which were believed to protect the body generally from serpents, worms, mildew, decay and putrefaction were laid with a lavish hand in, and upon, and about it, and between the bandages with which it was swathed. When men in Egypt began to lay amulets on their dead cannot be said, and it is equally impossible to say when the belief in the efficacy of such and such an amulet sprang into being; it seems clear, however, that certain amulets represent beliefs and superstitions so old that even the Egyptians were, at times, doubtful about their origin and meaning.

Amulets are of two kinds: (1) those which are inscribed with magical formulae, and (2) those which are not. In the earliest times formulae or prayers were recited over the amulets that were worn by the living or placed on the dead by priests or men set apart to perform religious services by the community; but it was not in the power of every man to employ them, and at a comparatively early date words of magical power and prayers were cut upon the amulets, which thus became possessed of a twofold power, that is to say, the power which was thought to be inherent in the substance of which the amulet was made, and that which lay in the words inscribed upon it. The earliest name for the formulae found upon amulets is *hekau*, and it was so necessary for the deceased to be provided with these hekau, or "words of power," that in the XVIth Century B.C., and probably more than a thousand years earlier, a special section was inserted in the Book of the Dead with the object of causing them to come to him from whatever place they were in, "swifter than greyhounds and quicker than light." The earliest Egyptian amulets known are pieces of green schist, of various shapes, animal and otherwise, which were laid upon the breast of the deceased; these are found in large numbers in the prehistoric or predynastic graves at several places in Egypt. It is most unlikely that they were made by the aboriginal inhabitants of Egypt, for, notwithstanding the various conjectures which have been made as to their object and use, it is pretty certain that, as M. J. de Morgan said, they "belong to the cult." According to this writer their use was exceedingly widespread until the end of the neolithic period, but with the advent of the people whom we call Egyptians they become very rare. In the subsequent period the animal forms disappear, and their place is taken by plaques of schist, rectangular in shape, upon which are inscribed, in rough outline, figures of animals, etc. The theory that these objects were intended as whetstones, or as slabs upon which to rub down paint, will not hold, for the reasons which M. J. de Morgan has given. Moreover, in the green stone scarab which was laid upon the breast of the deceased in dynastic times, we probably have a survival of the green schist amulet of predynastic times in Egypt, both as regards the object with which it was made and the material. But the custom of writing hekau, or words of power, upon papyrus is almost as old as that of writing them upon stone, and we see from the inscription on the walls of the corridors and chambers of the pyramid of Unas, king of Egypt about B.C. 3300, that a "book with words of magical power" was buried with him. Elsewhere we are told that the book which Teta, king of Egypt about B.C. 3266, had with him "hath effect upon the heart of the gods"; and there is no doubt that the object of every religious text ever written on tomb, stele, amulet, coffin, papyrus, etc., was to bring the gods under the power of the deceased, so that he might be able to compel them to do his will.

1. THE AMULET OF THE HEART

The heart was not only the seat of the power of life, but also the source of both good and evil thoughts; and it sometimes typified the conscience. It was guarded after death with special care, and was mummified separately, and then, with the lungs, was preserved in a jar which was placed under the protection of the god Tuamutef. Its preservation was considered to be of such importance that a text was introduced into the Book of the Dead at an early period, with the view of providing the deceased with a heart in the place of that which had been removed in the process of mummification. The text reads:-

"May my heart be with me in the House of Hearts! May my breast be with me in the House of Hearts! May my heart be with me, and may it rest there, or I shall not eat of the cakes of Osiris on the eastern side of the Lake of Flowers, neither shall I have a boat wherein to go down the Nile, nor another wherein to go up, nor shall I be able to sail down the Nile with thee. May my mouth [be given] to me that I may speak therewith, and my two legs to walk therewith, and my two hands and arms to overthrow my foe. May the doors of heaven be opened unto me;

may Seb, the prince of the gods, open wide his two jaws unto me; may he open my two eyes which are blindfolded; may he cause me to stretch apart my two legs which are bound together; and may Anpu (Anubis) make my thighs to be firm so that I may stand upon them. May the goddess Sekhet make me to rise so that I may ascend into heaven, and may that which I command in the House of the Ka of Ptah be done. I shall understand with my heart, I shall gain the mastery over my heart, I shall gain the mastery over my two hands, I shall gain the mastery over my legs, I shall have the power to do whatsoever my ka (i.e., double) pleaseth. My soul shall not be fettered to my body at the gates of the underworld, but I shall enter in and come forth in peace."

When the deceased had uttered these words, it was believed that he would at once obtain the powers which he wished to possess in the next world; and when he had gained the mastery over his heart, the heart, the double, and the soul had the power to go where they wished and to do what they pleased. The mention of the god Ptah and of his consort Sekhet indicates that the Chapter was the work of the priests of Memphis, and that the ideas embodied in it are of great antiquity. According to the Papyrus of

Nekhtu-Amen, the amulet of the heart, which is referred to in the above Chapter, was to be made of lapis-lazuli, and there is no doubt that this stone was believed to possess certain qualities which were beneficial to those who wore it. It will also be remembered that, according to one tradition, the text of the LXIVth Chapter of the Book of the Dead was found written in letters of lapis lazuli in the reign of Hesep-ti, king of Egypt about B.C. 4300, and the way in which the fact is mentioned in the Rubric to the Chapter proves that special importance was attached to it.

But although a heart might be given to a man by means of the above Chapter, it was necessary for the deceased to take the greatest care that it was not carried off from him by a monster, who was part man and part beast, and who went about seeking for hearts to carry away. To prevent such a calamity no less than seven Chapters of the Book of the Dead (Nos. XXVII., XXVIII., XXIX., XXIXA, XXX., XXXA, and XXXB) were written. The XXVIIth Chapter was connected with a heart amulet made of a white, semi-transparent stone, and reads:-

"Hail, ye who carry away hearts! Hail, ye who steal hearts, and who make the heart of a man to go through its transformations according to its deeds, let not what he hath done harm him before you!

Homage to you, O ye lords of eternity, ye possessors of ever lastingness, take ye not this heart of Osiris into your grasp, and cause ye not words of evil to spring up against it; for it is the heart of Osiris, and it belongeth unto him of many names, the mighty one whose words are his limbs, and who sendeth forth his heart to dwell in his body. The heart of Osiris is triumphant, and it is made new before the gods: he hath gained power over it, and he hath not been judged according to what he hath done. He hath gotten power over his own members. His heart obeyeth him, he is the lord thereof, it is in his body, and it shall never fall away therefrom. I, Osiris, victorious in peace, and triumphant in the beautiful Amenta and on the mountain of eternity, bid thee [O heart] to be obedient unto me in the underworld."

Another Chapter (XXIXB) was connected with a heart amulet made of carnelian, of which so many examples may be found in large museums; the text reads: "I am the Bennu, the soul of Râ, and the guide of the gods who are in the underworld. Their divine souls came forth upon earth to do the will of their doubles, let therefore the soul of the Osiris come forth to do the will of his double." The Bennu was also the soul of Osiris, and thus the amulet brought with it the protection of both Osiris and Râ.

But of all the Chapters which related to the heart, the most popular among the Egyptians was that which is commonly known as XXXB, and its importance from a religious point of view cannot be overstated. The antiquity of the Chapter is undoubted, for according to the Papyrus of Nu, a document of the early part of the XVIIIth dynasty, it dates from the time of Hesep-ti, king of Egypt about B.C. 4300, and it seems that it formed a pendant or supplement to the LXIVth Chapter, which professed to give the substance of all the "Chapters of Coming Forth by Day" in a single Chapter. In the rubric to the longer version of the Chapter, given in the same papyrus, Chapter XXXB is connected with Herutâtâf, the son of Khufu (Cheops), a man famed for wisdom, and it is there ordered that the words of it be recited over a hard, green stone scarab, which shall be laid in the breast of the deceased where the heart would ordinarily be; this amulet would then perform for him the "opening of the mouth," for the words of the Chapter would be indeed "words of power." From reciting the words of the Chapter over a scarab to engraving them upon it was but a step, and this step was taken as early as the IVth dynasty. The text is as follows:-

"My heart, my mother; my heart, my mother! My heart whereby I came into being! May naught stand up to oppose me at [my] judgment; may there be no opposition to me in the presence of the sovereign princes; may there be no parting of thee from me in the presence of him that keepeth the Balance! Thou art my double (ka), the dweller in my body, the god Khnemu who knitteth and strengtheneth my limbs. Mayest thou come forth into the place of happiness whither we go. May the Shenit, who form the conditions of the lives of men, not make my name to stink. Let it be satisfactory unto us, and let the listening be satisfactory unto us, and let there be joy of heart unto us at the weighing of words. Let not that which is false be uttered against me before the great god, the lord of Amentet. Verily how great shalt thou be when thou risest in triumph."

It was this Chapter which the deceased recited when he was in the Judgment Hall of Osiris, whilst his heart was being weighed in the Balance against the feather symbolic of right and truth. From certain papyri it seems as if the above words should, properly, be said by the deceased when he is being weighed against his own heart, a conception which is quite different from that of the judgment of the heart before the gods.

2. THE AMULET OF THE SCARAB

From what has been said above it will be seen that the amulet of the heart, which was connected with the most important and most popular of the Chapters for protecting the heart, was directed to be made in the form of the scarab at a very early date. We can trace the ideas which the Egyptians held about this insect as far back as the time of the building of the Pyramids, and there is no doubt that they represented beliefs which even at that early period were very old. The Egyptian seems to have reasoned thus: since the physical heart is taken from the body before mummification, and the body has need of another to act as the source of life and movement in its new life, another must be put in its place. But a stone heart, whether made of lapis lazuli or carnelian, is only a stone heart after all, and even though by means of prayers properly recited it prevents the physical heart from being carried off by "those who plunder hearts," it possesses nothing of itself which can be turned to account in giving new life and being to the body on which it lies. But the scarab or beetle itself possesses remarkable powers, and if a figure of the scarab be made, and the proper words of power be written upon it, not only protection of the dead physical heart, but also new life and existence will be given to him to whose body it is attached. Moreover, the scarab was the type and symbol of the god Khepera, the invisible power of creation which propelled the sun across the sky. The particular beetle chosen by the Egyptians to copy for amulets belongs to the family of dung-feeding Lamellicorns which live in tropical countries. The species are generally of a black hue, but amongst them are to be found some adorned with the richest metallic colours. A remarkable peculiarity exists in the structure and situation of the hind legs, which are placed so near the extremity of the body, and so far from each other, as to give the insect a most extraordinary appearance when walking. This peculiar formation is, nevertheless, particularly serviceable to its possessors in rolling the balls of excrementitious matter in which they enclose their eggs. These balls are at first irregular and soft, but, by degrees, and during the process of rolling along, become rounded and harder; they are propelled by means of the hind legs. Sometimes these balls are an inch and a half or two inches in diameter, and in rolling them along the beetles stand almost upon their beads, with the heads turned from the balls. These manœuvres have for their object the burying of the balls in holes, which the insects have previously dug for their reception; and it is upon the dung thus deposited that the larvæ, when hatched, feed. It does not appear that these beetles have the ability to distinguish their own balls, as they will seize upon those belonging to another, in the case of their having lost their own; indeed, it is said that several of them occasionally assist in rolling the same ball. The males as well as the females assist in rolling the pellets. They fly during the hottest part of the day.

Among the ancients several curious views were held about the scarab, whether of the type *scarabæus sacer* or the *ateuchus Ægyptiorium*, and Ælian, Porphyry, and Horapollo declared that no female scarab existed. The last named writer stated that the scarab denoted "only begotten," because it was a creature self-produced, being unconceived by a female. He goes on to say that, having made a ball of dung, the beetle rolls it from east to west, and having dug a hole, he buries it in it for eight and twenty days; on the twenty-ninth day he opens the ball, and throws it into the water, and from it the scarabæi come forth. The fact that the scarab flies during the hottest part of the day made the insect to be identified with the sun, and the ball of eggs to be compared to the sun itself. The unseen power of God, made manifest under the form of the god Khepera, caused the sun to roll across the sky, and the act of rolling gave to the scarab its name *kheper, i.e.,* "he who rolls." The sun contained the germs of all life, and as the insect's ball contained the germs of the young scarabs it was identified also with the sun as a creature which produced life in a special way. Now, the god Khepera also represented inert but living matter, which was about to begin a course of existence, and at a very early period he was considered to be a god of the resurrection; and since the scarab was identified with him that insect became at once the symbol of the god and the type of the resurrection. But the dead human body, from one aspect, contained the germ of life, that is to say, the germ of the spiritual body, which was called into being by means of the prayers that were recited and the ceremonies that were performed on the day of the funeral; from this point of view the insect's egg ball and the dead body were identical. Now, as the insect had given potential life to its eggs in the ball, so, it was thought, would a model of the scarab, itself the symbol of the god Khepera, also give potential life to the dead body upon which it was placed, always provided that the proper "words of power" were first said over it or written upon it. The idea of "life" appears to have attached itself to the scarab from time immemorial in Egypt and the Eastern Sûdân, for to this day the insect is dried, pounded, and mixed with water, and then drunk by women who believe it to be an unfailing specific for the production of large families. In ancient days when a man wished to drive away the effects of every kind of sorcery and incantations he might do so by cutting off the head and wings of a large beetle, which he boiled and laid in oil. The head and wings were then warmed up and steeped in the oil of the *âpnent* serpent, and when they had been once more boiled the man was to drink the mixture.

The amulet of the scarab has been found in Egypt in untold thousands, and the varieties are exceedingly numerous. They are made of green basalt, green granite, limestone, green marble, blue paste, blue glass, purple, blue and green glazed porcelain, etc.; and the words of power are usually cut in outline on the base. In rare instances, the scarab has a human face or head, and sometimes the backs are inscribed with figures of the boat of Râ, of the *Bennu* bird, "the soul of Râ," and of the eye of Horus. The green stone scarabs are often set in gold, and have a band of gold across and down the back where the wings join; sometimes the whole back is gilded, and sometimes the base is covered with a plate of gold upon which the words of power have been stamped or engraved. Occasionally the base of the scarab is made in the form of a heart, a fact which proves the closeness of the relationship which existed between the amulets of the heart and scarab. In late times, that is to say about B.C. 1200, large funeral scarabs were set in pylon-shaped pectorals, made of porcelain of various colours, upon which the boat of the Sun was either traced in colours or worked in relief, and the scarab is placed so as to appear to be carried in the boat; on the left stands Isis and on the right Nephthys. The oldest green stone funeral scarab known to me is in the British Museum (No. 29,224); it was found at Kûrna near Thebes and belongs to the period of the XIth dynasty, about B.C. 2600. The name of the man for whom it was made (he appears to have been an official of the Temple of Amen) was traced on it in light coloured paint which was afterwards varnished; there are no "words of power" on this interesting object.

When once the custom of burying scarabs with the bodies of the dead became recognized, the habit of wearing them as ornaments by the living came into fashion, and as a result scarabs of almost every sort and kind may be found by the thousand in many collections, and it is probable that the number of varieties of them was only limited by the ability of those who manufactured them in ancient days to invent new sorts. The use of the scarab amulet passed into Western Asia and into several countries which lay on the Mediterranean, and those who wore it seem to have attached to it much the same idea as its early inventors, the Egyptians. From a Greek magical papyrus translated by Goodwin we may see that certain solemn ceremonies were performed over a scarab before it was worn, even in the period of the rule of the Greeks and Romans. Thus about the "ring of Horus" and the "ceremony of the beetle" we are told to take a beetle, sculptured as described below, and to place it on a paper table, and under the table there shall be a pure linen cloth; under it put some olive wood, and set on the middle of the table a small censer wherein myrrh and kyphi shall be offered. And have at hand a small vessel of chrysolite into which ointment of lilies, or myrrh, or cinnamon, shall be put, and take the ring and lay it in the ointment, having first made it pure and clean, and offer it up in the censer with kyphi and myrrh; leave the ring for three days, and take it out and put it in a safe place. At the celebration let there lie near at hand some pure loaves, and such fruits as are in season, and having made another sacrifice upon vine sticks, during the sacrifice take the ring out of the ointment, and anoint thyself with the unction from it. Thou shalt anoint thyself early in the morning, and turning towards the east shalt pronounce the words written below. The beetle shall be carved out of a precious emerald; bore it and pass a gold wire through it, and beneath the beetle carve the holy Isis, and having consecrated it as above written, use it. The proper days for the celebration were the 7th, 9th, 10th, 12th, 14th, 16th, 21st, 24th, and 25th, from the beginning of the month; on other days abstain. The spell to be recited began, "I am

Thoth," the inventor and founder of medicines and letters; "come to me, thou that art under the earth, rise up to me, thou great spirit."

3. THE AMULET OF THE BUCKLE

This amulet represents the buckle of the girdle of Isis, and is usually made of carnelian, red jasper, red glass, and of other substances of a red colour; it is sometimes made of gold, and of substances covered with gold. It is always associated with the CLVIth Chapter of the Book of the Dead, which is frequently inscribed upon it, and which reads:-

"The blood of Isis, and the strength of Isis, and the words of power of Isis shall be mighty to act as powers to protect this great and divine being, and to guard him from him that would do unto him anything that he holdeth in abomination."

But before the buckle was attached to the neck of the deceased, where the rubric ordered it to be placed, it had to be dipped in water in which *ânkham* flowers had been steeped; and when the words of the Chapter of the Buckle given above had been recited over it, the amulet brought to the deceased the protection of the blood of Isis, and of her words of power. It will be remembered that she raised the dead body of Osiris by means of her words of power, and there is a legend to the effect that she smote the Sun-god Râ with severe sickness by the magical power which she possessed. Another object of the buckle was to give the deceased access to every place in the underworld, and to enable him to have "one hand towards heaven, and one hand towards earth."

4. THE AMULET OF THE TET.

This amulet probably represents the tree trunk in which the goddess Isis concealed the dead body of her husband, and the four cross-bars indicate the four cardinal points; it became a symbol of the highest religious importance to the Egyptians, and the setting up of the Tet at Busiris, which symbolized the reconstituting of the body of Osiris, was one of the most solemn of all the ceremonies performed in connexion with the worship of Osiris. The Tet represents neither the mason's table nor a Nilometer, as some have thought, It is always associated with the CLVth Chapter of the Book of the Dead, which reads:-

"Rise up thou, O Osiris! Thou hast thy backbone, O Still-Heart! Thou hast the fastenings of thy neck and

back, O Still-Heart! Place thou thyself upon thy base,
I put water beneath thee, and I bring unto thee a Tet
of gold that thou mayest rejoice therein."

Like the buckle, the Tet had to be dipped in the water
in which ânkham flowers had been steeped, and laid upon
the neck of the deceased, to whom it gave the power to
reconstitute the body and to become a perfect KHU (*i.e.*,
spirit) in the underworld. On coffins the right hand of the
deceased grasps the buckle, and the left the Tet; both are
made of wood, notwithstanding the fact that the rubric to
the Chapter of the Te orders the Tet to be made of gold.

5. THE AMULET OF THE PILLOW

This amulet is a model of the pillow which is found placed
under the neck of the mummy in the coffin, and its object
is to "lift up" and to protect the head of the deceased; it
is usually made of hæmatite, and is inscribed with the text
of the CLXVIth Chapter of the Book of the Dead, which
reads:-

"Thou art lifted up, O sick one that liest prostrate.
They lift up thy head to the horizon, thou art raised
up, and dost triumph by reason of what hath been

done for thee. Ptah hath overthrown thine enemies,
which was ordered to be done for thee. Thou art
Horus, the son of Hathor, ... who givest back the
head after the slaughter. Thy head shall not be carried
away from thee after [the slaughter], thy head shall
never, never be carried away from thee."

6. THE AMULET OF THE VULTURE

This amulet was intended to cause the power of Isis as the "divine mother" to be a protection for the deceased, and was made of gold in the form of a vulture hovering in the air with outstretched wings and holding in each talon the symbol of "life" ☥ and was placed on the neck on the day of the funeral. With this amulet the CLVIIth Chapter of the Book of the Dead was associated, and it was ordered by the rubric to it to be recited over it; this text reads:-

"Isis cometh and hovereth over the city, and she
goeth about seeking the secret habitations of Horus
as he emergeth from his papyrus swamps, and she
raiseth up his shoulder which is in evil case. He is
made one of the company in the divine boat, and the
sovereignty of the whole world is decreed for him.
He hath warred mightily, and he maketh his deeds

to be remembered; he hath made the fear of him to exist and awe of him to have its being. His mother the mighty lady, protecteth him, and she hath transferred her power unto him." The first allusion is to the care which Isis shewed for Horus when she was bringing him up in the papyrus swamps, and the second to his combat with Set, whom he vanquished through the might of Isis.

7. THE AMULET OF THE COLLAR OF GOLD.

This amulet was intended to give the deceased power to free himself from his swathings; it is ordered by the rubric to the CLVIIIth Chapter of the Book of the Dead to be placed on his neck on the day of the funeral, and to be made of gold. The text of the Chapter reads:-

"O my father, my brother, my mother Isis, I am unswathed, and I see. I am one of those who are unswathed and who see the god Seb." This amulet is very rare, and appears to have been the expression of beliefs which grew up in the period of the XXVIth dynasty, about B.C. 550.

8. THE AMULET OF THE PAPYRUS SCEPTRE.

This amulet was intended to give the deceased vigour and renewal of youth; it was made of mother-of-emerald, or of light green or blue porcelain, and, when the words of the CLIXth Chapter of the Book of the Dead had been recited over it, it was placed on his neck on the day of the funeral. In the XXVIth dynasty and later it seems as if the amulet represented the power of Isis, who derived it from her father, the husband of Renenet, the goddess of abundant harvests and food. At an earlier period, judging from the text of the CLXth Chapter, the amulet is put by the god Thoth into the hands of the deceased, who says, "It is in sound state, and I am in sound state; it is not injured, and I am not injured; it is not worn away, and I am not worn away."

9. THE AMULET OF THE SOUL.

This amulet was made of gold inlaid with precious stones in the form of a human-headed hawk, and, when the words of the LXXXIXth Chapter of the Book of the Dead had been recited over it, it was directed by the rubric to the Chapter to be placed upon the breast of the deceased. The object of the amulet is apparent from the text in which the deceased is made to say, "Hail, thou god Anniu! Hail, thou god Pehrer, who dwellest in thy hall! Grant thou that my soul may come unto me from wheresoever it may be. If it would tarry, then let my soul be brought unto me from wheresoever it may be… . Let me have possession of my soul and of my spirit, and let me be true of voice with them wheresoever they may be… . Hail, ye gods, who tow along the boat of the lord of millions of years, who bring it above the underworld, and who make it to travel over Nut, who make souls to enter into their spiritual bodies, … grant that the soul of the Osiris "may come forth before the gods, and that it may be true of voice with you in the east of the sky, and follow unto the place where it was yesterday, and enjoy twofold peace in Amentet. May it look upon its natural body, may it rest upon its spiritual body, and may its body neither perish nor suffer corruption for ever!" Thus the amulet of the soul was intended to enable the soul both to unite with the mummified body, and to be with its spirit (*khu*) and spiritual body at will.

10. THE AMULET OF THE LADDER.

In tombs of the Ancient and Middle Empires small objects of wood and other substances in the form of ladders have often been found, but the signification of them is not always apparent. From the texts inscribed upon the walls of the corridors and chambers of the pyramids of Unas, Teta, Pepi, and other early kings, it is clear that the primitive Egyptians believed that the floor of heaven, which also formed the sky of this world, was made of an immense plate of iron, rectangular in shape, the four corners of which rested upon four pillars which served to mark the cardinal points. On this plate of iron lived the gods and the blessed dead, and it was the aim of every good Egyptian to go there after death. At certain sacred spots the edge of the plate was so near the tops of the mountains that the deceased might easily clamber on to it and so obtain admission into heaven, but at others the distance between it and the earth was so great that he needed help to reach it. There existed a belief that Osiris himself experienced some difficulty of getting up to the iron plate, and that it was only by means of the ladder which his father Râ provided that he at length ascended into heaven. On one side of the ladder stood Râ, and on the other stood Horus, the son of Isis, and each god assisted Osiris to mount it. Originally the two guardians of the ladder were Horus the Elder and Set, and there are several references in the early texts to the help which they rendered to the deceased, who was, of course, identified with the god Osiris. But, with a view either of reminding these gods of their supposed duty, or of compelling them to do it, the model of a ladder was often placed on or near the dead body in the tomb, and a special composition was prepared which had the effect of making the ladder become the means of the ascent of the deceased into heaven. Thus in the text written for Pepi the deceased is made to address the ladder in these words: "Homage to thee, O divine Ladder! Homage to thee, O Ladder of Set! Stand thou upright, O divine Ladder! Stand thou upright, O Ladder of Set! Stand thou upright, O Ladder of Horus, whereby Osiris came forth into heaven when he made use of his magical power upon Râ.... For Pepi is thy son, and Pepi is Horus, and thou hast given birth unto Pepi even as thou hast given birth unto the god who is the lord of the Ladder (*i.e.*, Horus); and thou shalt give unto Pepi the Ladder of the god (*i.e.*, Horus), thou shalt give unto him the Ladder of the god Set whereby this Pepi shall come forth into heaven when he shall have made use of his magical power upon Râ. O 'thou god of those whose doubles (*kau*) pass onwards, (when the Eye of Horus soareth upon the wing of 'Thoth on the east side of the divine Ladder (or Ladder of God), O men whose bodies [would go] into heaven, Pepi is the Eye of Horus, and when the 'Eye turneth itself to any place where he is, Pepi goeth side by side with the Eye of Horus, and O ye who are the brethren of the gods, rejoice ye that Pepi journeyeth among you. And the brethren of Pepi who axe the gods shall be glad when they meet Pepi, even as Horus is glad when he meeteth his Eye. He hath placed his Eye before his father Seb, and every god and every spirit stretcheth out his hand towards Pepi when he cometh forth into heaven from the Ladder. Pepi hath need neither to 'plough the earth,' nor to 'collect the offering'; and he hath (need neither to go to the Hall which is in Annu (Heliopolis), nor to the Hall of the Morning which is in Annu; for that which he seeth and that which he heareth shall feed him and nourish him when he appeareth in heaven from the Ladder. Pepi riseth like the uraeus on the forehead of Set, and every god and every spirit stretcheth out his hand to Pepi on the Ladder. Pepi hath gathered together his bones, be hath collected his flesh, and he hath gone quickly into heaven by means of the two fingers of the god of the Ladder (*i.e.*, Horus). Elsewhere the gods Khonsu, Sept, etc., are invoked to bring the ladder to Pepi, and the ladder itself is adjured to come with its name, and in another place we read, Homage to thee, O thou Ladder that supportest the golden vase of the Spirits of Pe and the Spirits of Nekhen, stretch out thy hand to this Pepi, and let him take his seat between the two great gods who (care in the place of this Pepi; take him by the hand and lead him towards Sekhet-Hetep (*i.e.*, the Elysian Fields), and let him take his seat among the stars which are in the sky."

In the Theban Recension of the Book of the Dead the importance of the ladder is also seen, for in Chapter CXLIX. the deceased says, "I set up a Ladder among the gods, and I am a divine being among them"; and in Chapter CLIII. he says, "The Osiris Nu shall come forth upon your Ladder which Râ hath made for him, and Horus and Set shall grasp him firmly by the hand." Finally, when the custom of placing a model of the ladder in the tomb fell into disuse, the priests provided for the necessity of the dead by painting a ladder on the papyri that were inscribed with the texts from the Book of the Dead and were buried with them.

11. THE AMULET OF THE TWO FINGERS.

This amulet is intended to represent the two fingers, index and medius, which the god Horus employed in helping his father Osiris up the ladder into heaven, as has been described above; it is found in the interior of mummies and is usually made of obsidian or hæmatite.

12. THE AMULET OF THE EYE OF HORUS.

The Eye of Horus amulet, or Utchat, is one of the commonest of all, and its use seems to have been universal at all periods.

It was made of gold, silver, granite, hæmatite, carnelian, lapis-lazuli, porcelain, wood, etc., although the rubric of a late Chapter of the Book of the Dead directs that the amulet should be made either of lapis lazuli or of *mak* stone. The Utchat is of two kinds, one facing to the left and the other to the right, and together they represent the two eyes of Horus, one of which, according to an ancient text, was white and the other black; from another point of view one Utchat represents the Sun and the other the Moon, or Râ and Osiris respectively. But speaking generally, when the Egyptians wore the Utchat as an amulet they intended it to bring to them the blessings of strength, vigour, protection, safety, good health, and the like, and they had in their minds the Eye of Horus, probably the white one, or the Sun. In religious texts the expression *meh Utchat, i.e.,* the "filling of the Utchat," is often used, and from many considerations it is clear that we must understand it to refer to the Sun at the summer solstice; thus the amulet seems to have been intended to bring to its wearer strength and health similar to that of the Sun at the season of the year when it is most powerful. In the CLXVIIth Chapter of the Book of the Dead the deceased is made to say, "The god Thoth hath brought the Utchat, and he hath made it to rest after it departed, O Râ. It was grievously afflicted by the storm, but Thoth made it to rest after it departed out of the storm. I am sound, and it is sound; I am sound, and it is sound; and Nebseni, the lord of piety, is sound." To obtain the full benefit of the Utchat amulet for the deceased it was obligatory to make one in lapis-lazuli and to plate it with gold, and then to offer to it offerings at the summer solstice; another had then to be made of jasper and, if after the specified Chapter (CXL.) had been recited over it, it was laid on any part of the body of the deceased, he would become a god and take his place in the boat of Râ. At this solstice twelve altars had to be lighted, four for Râ-Temu, four for the Utchat, and four for the other gods who had been mentioned in the Chapter. An interesting example of the use of the *utchat* occurs in a Greek spell for the discovery of a thief written as late as the IVth century of our era. In it we are told to "take the herb *khelkbei* and *bugloss*, press out the juice and burn the crushed leaves and mix the ashes with the juice. Anoint and write upon a wall Khoô with these materials. And take a common piece of wood, and cut a hammer out of it, and strike with it upon the ear, pronouncing this spell:--'I adjure thee by the holy names, render up the thief, who has carried away such [and such] a thing Khalkhak, Khalkoum, Khiam, Khar, Khroum, Zbar, Bêri, Zbarkom, Khrê, Kariôb, Pharibou, and by the terrible names αεεηηιιιοοοοουυυυυυωωωωωωω {Greek *aeehhhiiiiooooouuuuuuwwwwwww*}'" Following these words we have a picture of the utchat with an arrangement of certain vowels on each side of it thus:

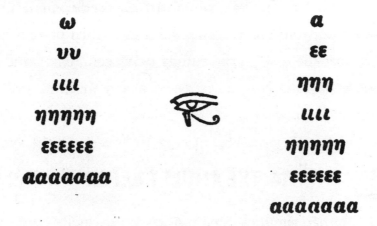

ω   α

υυ   εε

ιιιι   ηηη

ηηηηη   ιιιι

εεεεε   ηηηηη

αααααα   εεεεε

                                   αααααα

The spell continues, "Render up the thief who has stolen such [and such] a thing: as long as I strike the ear with this hammer, let the eye of the thief be smitten and inflamed until it betrays him.' Saying these words strike with the hammer."

13. THE AMULET OF "LIFE" (ÂNKH).

The object which is represented by this amulet is unknown, and of all the suggestions which have been made concerning it none is more unlikely than that which would give it a phallic origin. Whatever it may represent, it certainly symbolizes "life"; every god carries it, and it seems, even in the earliest times, to be a conventional representation of some object which in the remotest period had been used as an amulet. In the Papyrus of Ani (2nd edit., plate 2) the Ânkh rises from the Tet, and the arms which project from it support the disk of the sun as here seen. This amulet is made of various substances, and was chiefly employed as a pendant of a necklace.

14. THE AMULET NEFER.

This amulet signifies "happiness, good luck," etc., and represents a musical instrument; it was made of carnelian, red stone, red porcelain, and the like, and was a very favourite form for the pendants of necklaces and strings of beads.

15. THE AMULET OF THE SERPENT'S HEAD.

This amulet was placed on the dead body to keep it from being bitten by snakes in the underworld or tomb. It is made of red stone, red jasper, red paste, and carnelian. As the goddess Isis is often typified by a serpent, and red is a colour peculiar to her, it seems as if the idea underlying the use of this amulet was to vanquish the snakes in the tomb by means of the power of the great snake-goddess

Isis. This power had been transferred to it by means of the words of the XXXIVth Chapter of the Book of the Dead, which are often inscribed upon it. The text reads: "O Serpent! I am the flame which shineth upon the Opener of hundreds of thousands of years, and the standard of the god Tenpu," or as others say, "the standard of young plants and flowers. Depart ye from me, for I am the divine Lynx." Some have thought that the snake's head represents the serpent which surmounts the ram's head on the *urhekau* instrument used in performing the ceremony of "Opening the mouth."

16. THE AMULET OF THE MENAT.

This amulet was in use in Egypt as early as the VIth dynasty, and it was worn or held or carried with the sistrum by gods, kings, priests, priestesses, etc.; usually it is held in the hand, but it is often worn on the neck. Its object was to bring joy and health to the wearer, and it was believed to possess magical properties; it represented nutrition and strength, and the might of the male and female organs of generation, mystically considered, was supposed to be united therein. The amulet is made in bronze, stone, porcelain, and other substances, and when laid upon the body of the dead brought to it the power of life and reproduction.

17. THE AMULET OF THE SAM.

This amulet is probably intended to represent an organ of the human body, and its use is very ancient; it is made of lapis-lazuli and other hard stone substances, and in the late period is often found in the swathings of mummies. Its primary meaning is "union," and refers to animal pleasure.

18. THE AMULET OF THE SHEN.

This amulet is intended to represent the sun's orbit, and it became the symbol of an undefined period of time, *i.e.*, eternity; it was laid upon the body of the dead with the view of giving to it life which should endure as long as the sun revolved in its orbit in the heavens. In the picture of the mummy chamber the goddesses Isis and Nephthys are seen kneeling and resting their hands on *shen*. Figures of the *shen* were painted upon stelae, coffins, etc.; as an amulet it is commonly made of lapis lazuli or carnelian. The amulet of the cartouche has been supposed to be nothing more than *shen* elongated, but it probably refers to the ordinary meaning of "name."

19. THE AMULET OF THE STEPS.

This amulet seems to have two meanings: to lift up to heaven, and the throne of Osiris. According to one legend, when the god Shu wished to lift up the goddess Nut from the embrace of the god Seb, so that her body, supported by her stretched-out arms and legs, might form the sky, he found that he was not tall enough to do so; in this difficulty he made use of a flight of steps, and having mounted to the top of these he found himself able to perform his work. In the fourth section of the Elysian Fields three such flights of steps are depicted. In the XXIInd Chapter of the Book of the Dead the deceased prays that he "may have a portion with him who is on the top of the steps," *i.e.*, Osiris, and in funeral vignettes this god is seen seated upon the top of a flight of steps and holding his usual symbols of sovereignty and dominion. The amulet of the Steps is usually made of green or blue glazed porcelain.

20. THE AMULET OF THE FROG.

This amulet is typical of teeming life and of the resurrection. The frog-headed goddess Heqt, the wife of Khnemu, was associated with the resurrection, and this amulet, when laid upon the body of the dead, was intended to transfer to it her power. The frog is often represented on the upper part of the Greek and Roman terra-cotta lamps which are found in Egypt, and on one of them written in Greek is the legend, "I am the resurrection."

The amulets described above are those which are most commonly found in the tombs and on mummies, but a few others are also known, *e.g.*, the White crown of the South, the Red crown of the North, the horizon, or place where the sun rises, an angle, typifying protection, the horns, disk, and plumes, or the plummet, etc. Besides these, any ring, or pendant, or ornament, or any object whatsoever, upon which was inscribed the name of a god or his emblem, or picture, became an amulet with protective powers; and it seems that these powers remained active as long as the substance lasted and as long as the name, or emblem, or picture, was not erased from it. The use of amulets was common in Egypt from the earliest times to the Roman Period, and when the Egyptians embraced Christianity, they, in common with the Gnostics and semi-Christian sects, imported into their new faith many of the views and beliefs which their so-called heathen ancestors had held, and with them the use of the names of ancient Egyptian gods, and goddesses, and demons, and formulae, which they employed in much the same way as they were employed in the days of old.

CHAPTER III
MAGICAL FIGURES

IT has been said above that the name or the emblem or the picture of a god or demon could become an amulet with power to protect him that wore it, and that such power lasted as long as the substance of which it was made lasted, if the name, or emblem, or picture was not erased from it. But the Egyptians went a step further than this, and they believed that it was possible to transmit to the *figure* of any man, or woman, or animal, or living creature, the soul of the being which it represented, and its qualities and attributes. The statue of a god in a temple contained the spirit of the god which it represented, and from time immemorial the people of Egypt believed that every statue and every figure possessed an indwelling spirit. When the Christianized Egyptians made their attacks on the "idols of the heathen" they proved that they possessed this belief, for they always endeavoured to throw down the statues of the gods of the Greeks and Romans, knowing that if they were once shattered the spirits which dwelt in them would have no place wherein to dwell, and would thereby be rendered homeless and powerless. It will be remembered that it is stated in the Apocryphal Gospels that when the Virgin Mary and her Son arrived in Egypt there "was a movement and quaking throughout all the land, and all the idols fell down from their pedestals and were broken in pieces." Then all the priests and nobles went to a certain priest with whom "a devil used to speak from out of the idol," and they asked him the meaning of these things; and when he had explained to them that the footstep of the son of the "secret and hidden god" had fallen upon the land of Egypt, they accepted his counsel and made a figure of this god. The Egyptians acknowledged that the new god was greater than all their gods together, and they were quite prepared to set up a statue of him because they believed that in so doing they would compel at least a portion of the spirit of the "secret and hidden god" to come and dwell in it. In the following pages we shall endeavour to describe the principal uses which the Egyptians made of the figures of gods, and men, and beasts, to which magical powers had been imparted by means of the performance of certain symbolic ceremonies and the recital of certain words of power; and how they could be employed to do both good and evil.

One of the earliest instances of the use of a magical figure is related in the Westcar Papyrus, where we read that Prince Khâf-Râ told Khufu (Cheops) a story of an event which had happened in the time of Neb-ka or Neb-kau-Ed, a king of the IIIrd dynasty, who reigned about B.C. 3830. It seems that this king once paid a visit to one of his high officials called Âba-aner, whose wife fell violently in love with one of the soldiers in the royal train. This lady sent her tirewoman to him with the gift of a chest of clothes, and apparently she made known to him her mistress's desire, for he returned with her to Âba-aner's house. There he saw the wife and made an appointment to meet her in a little house which was situated on her husband's estate, and she gave instructions to one of the stewards of Âba-aner to prepare it for the arrival of herself and her lover. When all had been made ready she went to the house and stayed there the whole day drinking and making love with the man until sunset; and when the evening had come he rose up and went down to the river and the tirewoman bathed him in the water thereof. But the steward, who had made ready the house, declared that he must make the matter known unto his master, and on the following morning as soon as it was light, he went to Âba-aner and related to him everything which had happened. The official made no answer to his servant's report, but ordered him to bring him certain materials and his box made of ebony and precious metal. Out of the box he took a quantity of wax, which was, no doubt, kept there for purposes similar to that to which a portion of it was now to be put, and made a model of a crocodile seven spans long, and then reciting certain magical words over it, he said, "When the man cometh down to bathe in my waters seize thou him." Then, turning to the steward, he gave the wax crocodile to him and said, "When the man, according to his daily wont, cometh down to wash in the water thou shalt cast the crocodile in after him"; and the steward having taken the wax crocodile from his master went his way.

And again the wife of Âba-aner ordered the steward who had charge of the estate to make ready the house which was in the garden, "for," she said, "behold, I am coming to pass some time therein." So the house was made ready and provided with all good things, and she came with the man and passed some time with him there. Now when the evening was come the man went down to the water to wash according to his daily wont, and the steward went down after him and threw into the water the wax crocodile, which straightway turned into a living crocodile seven cubits (*i.e.*, about twelve feet) in length, and seized upon the man and dragged him down in the water.

Meanwhile Âba-aner tarried with his king Neb-kau-Râ for seven days, and the man remained in the depths of the water and had no air to breathe. And on the seventh day Âba-aner the *kher heb* went out with the king for a walk, and invited His Majesty to come and see for himself a wonderful thing which had happened to a man in his own days; so the king went with him. When they had come to the water Âba-aner adjured the crocodile, saying, "Bring hither the man," and the crocodile came out of the water bringing the man with him. And when the king remarked that the crocodile was a horrid looking monster, Âba-aner stooped down and took it up into his hand, when it straightway became a waxen crocodile as it was before. After these things Âba-aner related to the king what had happened between his wife and the man whom the crocodile had brought up out of the water, whereupon the king said to the crocodile, "Take that which is thine and begone"; and immediately the crocodile seized the man and sprang into the water with him, and disappeared in its depths. And by the royal command Âba-aner's wife was seized, and having been led to the north side of the palace was burnt, and her ashes were cast into the stream. Here then we have already in the IIIrd dynasty the existence of a belief that a wax crocodile, over which certain words had been said, could change itself into a living reptile at pleasure, and that a man could be made by the same means to live at the bottom of a stream for seven days without air. We may also notice that the great priestly official, the kher heb, was so much in the habit of performing such acts of magic that he kept in a room a box of materials and instruments always ready for the purpose; and, apparently, neither himself, nor his king, nor his servant, thought the working of magic inconsistent with his high religious office.

But at the time when Âba-aner was working magic by means of wax figures, probably to the harm and injury of his enemies, the priests were making provision for the happiness and well-being of the dead also by means of figures made of various substances. According to one very early belief the dead made their way to a region called Sekhet-Aaru, where they led a life which was not very different from that which they had led upon earth. From the pictures of this place which are painted on coffins of the XIth dynasty, we see that it was surrounded by streams of water, and that it was intersected by canals, and that, in fact, it was very much like an ordinary well-kept estate in the Delta. The beings who lived in this place, however, had the same wants as human beings, that is to say, they needed both food and drink, or bread-cakes and ale. The existence of bread and ale presupposed the existence of wheat and barley, and the production of these presupposed the tilling of the ground and the work of agricultural labourers. But the Egyptian had no wish to continue the labours of ploughing and reaping and preparing the ground for the new crops in the world beyond the grave, therefore he endeavoured to avoid this by getting the work done vicariously. If words of power said over a figure could make it to do evil, similarly words of power said over a figure could make it to do good. At first a formula was composed, the recital of which was supposed to relieve the deceased from the necessity of doing any work whatsoever, and when the deceased himself had said, "I lift up the hand of the man who is inactive. I have come from the city of Unnu (Hermopolis). I am the divine Soul which liveth, and I lead with me the hearts of the apes," his existence was thought to be without toil. But, since the inhabitants of Sekhet-Aaru needed food and drink, provision must be made for their production, and the necessary labours of the field must, in some manner, be performed. To meet the difficulty a small stone figure of the deceased was buried with him, but before it was laid in the tomb the priests recited over it the words of power which would cause it to do for the deceased whatever work he might be adjudged to perform in the kingdom of Osiris. Later, these words were inscribed upon the figure in hieroglyphics, and later still the figure was provided with representations of the rope basket, and plough, and flail, such as were employed by the Egyptian labourer in carrying field produce, and in ploughing, and in threshing grain. The formula or words of power which were inscribed on such figures varied at different periods, but one of the oldest, which was in use in the XVIIIth dynasty, makes the deceased say to the figure, which was called "Shabti":-

"O thou Shabti figure of the scribe Nebseni, if I be called, or if I be adjudged to do any work whatsoever of the labours which are to be done in the underworld by a man in his turn--behold, any obstacles (or opposition) to thee will be done away with there-- let the judgment fall upon thee instead of upon me always, in the matter of sowing the fields, of filling the water-courses with water, and of bringing the sands from the east to the west." After these words comes the answer by the figure, "Verily I am here, and [will do] whatsoever thou biddest me to do."

The Egyptians were most anxious to escape the labours of top-dressing the land, and of sowing the seed, a work which had to be done by a man standing in water in the sun, and the toilsome task of working the shadûf, or instrument for raising water from the Nile and turning it on to the land. In graves not one figure only is found, but several, and it is said that in the tomb of Seti I., king of Egypt about B.C. 1370, no less than seven hundred wooden ushabtiu inscribed with the VIth Chapter of the Book of the Dead, and covered with bitumen, were found. The use of the shabti figure continued unabated down to the Roman period, when boxes full of ill-shaped, uninscribed porcelain figures were buried in the tombs with the dead.

The next instance worth mentioning of the use of magical figures we obtain from the official account of a conspiracy against Rameses III., king of Egypt about B.C. 1200. It seems that a number of high officials, the Overseer of the Treasury included, and certain scribes, conspired together against this king apparently with the view of dethroning him. They took into their counsels a number of the ladies attached to the court (some think they belonged to the *harîm*), and the chief abode of these ladies became the headquarters of the conspirators. One official was charged with "carrying abroad their words to their mothers and sisters who were there to stir up men and to incite malefactors to do wrong to their lord"; another was charged with aiding and abetting the conspiracy by making himself one with the ringleaders; another was charged with being cognizant of the whole matter, and with concealing his knowledge of it; another with "giving ear to the conversation held by the men conspiring with the women of the Per-khent, and not bringing it forward against them," and so on. The conspiracy soon extended from Egypt to Ethiopia, and a military official of high rank in that country was drawn into it by his sister, who urged him to "Incite the men to commit crime, and do thou thyself come to do wrong to thy lord"; now the sister of this official was in the Per-khent, and so she was able to give her brother the latest information of the progress of the disaffection. Not content with endeavouring to dethrone the king by an uprising of both soldiers and civilians, Hui, a certain high official, who was the overseer of the [royal] cattle, bethought him of applying magic to help their evil designs, and with this object in view he went to some one who had access to the king's library, and he obtained from him a book containing formulae of a magical nature, and directions for working magic. By means of this book he obtained "divine power," and he became able to cast spells upon folk. Having gained possession of the book he next looked out for some place where he could carry on his magical work without interruption, and at length found one. Here he set to work to make figures of men in wax, and amulets inscribed with words of magical power which would provoke love, and these he succeeded in introducing into the royal palace by means of the official Athirmâ; and it seems as if those who took them into the palace and those who received them were under the magical influence of Hui. It is probable that the love philtres were intended for the use of the ladies who were involved in the conspiracy, but as to the object of the wax figures there is no doubt, for they were intended to work harm to the king. Meanwhile Hui studied his magical work with great diligence, and he succeeded in finding efficacious means for carrying out all the "horrible things and all the wickednesses which his heart could imagine"; these means he employed in all seriousness, and at length committed great crimes which were the horror of every god and goddess, and the punishment of such crimes was death. In another place Hui is accused of writing books or formulae of magical words, the effect of which would be to drive men out of their senses, and to strike terror into them; and of making gods of wax and figures of men of the same substance, which should cause the human beings whom they represented to become paralysed and helpless. But their efforts were in vain, the conspiracy was discovered, and the whole matter was carefully investigated by two small courts of enquiry, the members of which consisted, for the most part, of the king's personal friends; the king's orders to them were that "those who are guilty shall die by their own hands, and tell me nothing whatever about it." The first court, which consisted of six members, sat to investigate the offences of the husbands and relatives of the royal ladies, and those of the ladies themselves, but before their business was done three of them were arrested because it was found that the ladies had gained great influence over them, that they and the ladies had feasted together, and that they had ceased to be, in consequence, impartial judges. They were removed from their trusted positions before the king, and having been examined and their guilt clearly brought home to them, their ears and noses were cut off as a punishment and warning to others not to form friendships with the enemies of the king. The second court, which consisted of five members, investigated the cases of those who were charged with having "stirred up men and incited malefactors to do wrong to their lord," and having found them guilty they sentenced six of them to death, one by one, in the following terms:- "Pentaura, who is also called by another name. He was brought up on account of the offence which he had committed in connexion with his mother Thi when she formed a conspiracy with the women of the Per-khent, and because he had intent to do evil unto his lord. He was brought before the court of judges that he might receive sentence, and they found him guilty, and dismissed him to his own death, where he suffered death by his own hand." The wretched man Hui, who made wax figures and spells with the intent to inflict pain and suffering and death upon the king, was also compelled to commit suicide.

The above story of the famous conspiracy against Rameses III is most useful as proving that books of magic existed in the Royal Library, and that they were not mere treatises on magical practices, but definite works with detailed instructions to the reader how to perform the ceremonies which were necessary to make the formulae or words of power efficacious. We have now seen that wax figures were used both to do good and to do harm, from the IIIrd to the XXth dynasty, and that the ideas which the Egyptians held concerning them were much the same about B.C. 1200 as they were two thousand five hundred years earlier; we have also seen that the use of *ushabtiu* figures, which were intended to set the deceased free from the necessity of labour in the world beyond the grave, was widespread. That such figures were used in the pre-dynastic days when the Egyptians were slowly emerging into civilization from a state of semi-barbarism is not to be wondered at, and it need not surprise us that they existed as a survival in the early dynasties before the people generally had realized that the great powers of Nature, which they deified, could not be ruled by man and by his petty words and deeds, however mysterious and solemn. It is, however, very remarkable to find that the use of wax figures played a prominent part in certain of the daily services which were performed in the temple of the god Amen-Râ at Thebes, and it is still more remarkable that these services were performed at a time when the Egyptians were renowned among the nations of the civilized world for their learning and wisdom. One company of priests attached to the temple was employed in transcribing hymns and religious compositions in which the unity, power, and might of God were set forth in unmistakable terms, and at the same time another company was engaged in performing a service the object of which was to free the Sun, which was deified under the form of Râ, and was the type and symbol of God upon earth, from the attacks of a monster called Âpep!

It will be remembered that the XXXIXth Chapter of the Book of the Dead is a composition which was written with the object of defeating a certain serpent, to which many names are given, and of delivering the deceased from his attacks. In it we have a description of how the monster is vanquished, and the deceased says to him, "Râ maketh thee to turn back, O thou that art hateful to him; he looketh upon thee, get thee back. He pierceth thy head, he cutteth through thy face, he divideth thy head at the two sides of the ways, and it is crushed in his land; thy bones are smashed in pieces, thy members are hacked from off thee, and the god Aker hath condemned thee, O Âpep, thou enemy of Râ. Get thee back, Fiend, before the darts of his beams! Râ hath overthrown thy words, the gods have turned thy face backwards, the Lynx hath torn open thy breast, the Scorpion hath cast fetters upon thee, and Maât hath sent forth thy destruction. The gods of the south, and of the north, of the west, and of the east, have fastened chains upon him, and they have fettered him with fetters; the god Rekes hath overthrown him, and the god Hertit hath put him in chains." The age of this composition is unknown, but it is found, with variants, in many of the copies of the Book of the Dead which were made in the XVIIIth dynasty. Later, however, the ideas in it were developed, the work itself was greatly enlarged, and at the time of the Ptolemies it had become a book called "The Book of Overthrowing Âpep," which contained twelve chapters. At the same time another work bearing the same title also existed; it was not divided into chapters, but it contained two versions of the history of the Creation, and a list of the evil names of Âpep, and a hymn to Râ. Among the chapters of the former work was one entitled, "Chapter of putting the fire upon Âpep," which reads, "Fire be upon thee, Âpep, thou enemy of Râ! The Eye of Horus prevails over the accursed soul and shade of Âpep, and the flame of the Eye of Horus shall gnaw into that enemy of Râ; and the flame of the Eye of Horus shall consume all the enemies of the Mighty God, life! strength! health! both in death and in life. When Âpep is given to the flame," says the rubric, "thou shalt say these words of power:- Taste thou death, O Âpep, get thee back, retreat, O enemy of Râ, fall down, be repulsed, get back and retreat! I have driven thee back, and I have cut thee in pieces.

> Râ triumphs over Âpep. Taste thou death, Âpep.
> Râ triumphs over Âpep. Taste thou death, Âpep.
> Râ triumphs over Âpep. Taste thou death, Âpep.
> Râ triumphs over Âpep. Taste thou death, Âpep."

These last sentences were said four times, that is to say, once for each of the gods of the cardinal points. The text continues, "Back, Fiend, an end to thee! Therefore have I driven flame at thee, and therefore have I made thee to be destroyed, and therefore have I adjudged thee to evil. An end, an end to thee! Taste thou death! An end to thee! Thou shalt never rise again." Such are the words of power, and these are followed by the directions for performing the ceremony, which read thus:-

"If thou wouldst destroy Âpep, thou shalt say this chapter over a figure of Âpep which hath been drawn

in green colour upon a sheet of new papyrus, and over a wax figure of Âpep upon which his name hath been cut and inlaid with green colour; and thou shalt lay them upon the fire so that it may consume the enemy of Râ. And thou shalt put such a figure on the fire at dawn, and another at noon, and another at eventide when Râ setteth in the land of life, and another at midnight, and another at the eighth hour of the day, and another towards evening; [and if necessary] thou mayest do thus every hour during the day and the night, and on the days of the festivals and every day. By means of this Âpep, the enemy of Râ, shall be overthrown in the shower, for Râ shall shine and Âpep shall indeed be overthrown... And the papyrus and the figure "having been burnt in a fire made of khesau grass, the remains thereof shall be mixed with excrement and thrown upon a fire; thou shalt do this at the sixth hour of the night, and at dawn on the fifteenth day [of the month]. And when the figure of Âpep is placed in the fire thou shalt spit upon him several times each hour during the day, until the shadow turneth round. Thou shalt do these things when tempests rage in the east of the sky as Râ setteth, in order to prevent the coming onward of the storms. Thou shalt do this and so prevent the coming

*of a shower or a rain-storm, and thereby shall the sun
be made to shine."*

In another part of this book the reciter is told to say the
following "firmly with the mouth":- "Down upon thy face,
O Âpep, enemy of Râ! The flame which cometh forth from
the Eye of Horus advanceth against thee. Thou art thrust
down into the flame it of fire and it cometh against thee.
Its flame is deadly to thy soul, and to thy spirit, and to
thy words of power, and to thy body, and to thy shade.
The lady of fire prevaileth over thee, the flame pierceth thy
soul, it maketh an end of thy person, and it darteth into
thy form. The eye of Horus which is powerful against its
enemy hath cast thee down, it devoureth thee, the great
fire trieth thee, the Eye of Râ prevaileth over thee, the
flame devoureth thee, and what escapeth from it hath no
being. Get thee back, for thou art cut asunder, thy soul is
shrivelled up, thy accursed name is buried in oblivion, and
silence is upon it, and it hath fallen [out of remembrance].
Thou hast come to an end, thou hast been driven away,
and thou art forgotten, forgotten, forgotten," etc. To make
these words to be of effect the speaker is told to write the
names of Âpep upon a new papyrus and to burn it in the
fire either when Râ is rising, or at noon, or at sunset, etc.
In another part of the work, after a series of curses which

are ordered to be said over Âpep, the rubric directs that they shall be recited by a person who hath washed himself and is ceremonially clean, and when this has been done he is to write in green colour upon a piece of new papyrus the names of all the fiends who are in the train of Âpep, as well as those of their fathers, and mothers, and children. He must then make figures of all these fiends in wax, and having inscribed their names upon them, must tie them up with black hair, and then cast them on the ground and kick them with the left foot, and pierce them with a stone spear; this done they are to be thrown into the fire. More than once is it said, "It is good for a man to recite this book before the august god regularly," for the doing of it was believed to give great power "to him, both upon earth and in the underworld." Finally, after the names of Âpep are enumerated, be who would benefit by the knowledge of them is bidden to "make the figure of a serpent with his tail in his mouth, and having stuck a knife in his back, cast him down upon the ground and say, "Âpep, Fiend, Betet." Then, in order to destroy the fiends who are in the train of Âpep, other images or figures of them must be made with their hands tied behind them; these are to be called "Children of inactivity." The papyrus then continues, "Make another serpent with the face of a cat, and with a knife stuck in his back, and call it 'Hemhem' (Roarer).

Make another with the face of a crocodile, and with a knife stuck in his back, and call it 'Hauna-aru-her-hra.' Make another with the face of a duck, and with a knife stuck in his back, and call it 'Aluti.' Make another with the face of a white cat, and with a knife stuck in his back, and tie it up and bind it tightly, and call it 'Âpep the Enemy.'" Such are the means which the Egyptians adopted when they wanted to keep away rain and storm, thunder and lightning, and mist and cloud, and to ensure a bright clear sky wherein the sun might run his course.

Under the heading of "Magical Figures" must certainly be included the so-called Ptah-Seker-Ausar figure which is usually made of wood; it is often solid, but is sometimes made hollow, and is usually let into a rectangular wooden stand which may be either solid or hollow. The three gods or trinity of Ptah, Seker (Socharis), and Ausar (Osiris), are intended to represent the god of the sunrise (Ptah), the god of the night sun (Seker), and the god of the resurrection (Osiris). The name Ptah means "Opener," and is usually applied to the sun as the "opener" of the day; and the name Seker means "He who is shut in," that is to say, the night sun, who was regarded as the sun buried temporarily. Now the life of a man upon earth was identified with that of the sun; he "opened" or began his life as Ptah, and after death he was "shut in" or "coffined," like it also. But the sun rises again when the night is past, and, as it begins a new life with renewed strength and vigour, it became the type of the new life which the Egyptian hoped to live in the world beyond the grave. But the difficulty was how to obtain the protection of Ptah, Seker, and Osiris, and how to make them do for the man that which they did for themselves, and so secure their attributes. To attain this end a figure was fashioned in such a way as to include the chief characteristics of the forms of these gods, and was inserted in a rectangular wooden stand which was intended to represent the coffin or chest out of which the trinity Ptah-Seker-Ausar came forth. On the figure itself and on the sides of the stand were inscribed prayers on behalf of the man for whom it was made, and the Egyptian believed that these prayers caused the might and powers of the three gods to come and dwell in the wooden figure. But in order to make the stand of the figure as much like a coffin as possible, a small portion of the body of the deceased was carefully mummified and placed in it, and it was thought that if the three gods protected and preserved that piece, and if they revivified it in due season, the whole body would be protected, and preserved, and revivified. Frequently, especially in the late period, a cavity was made in the side of the stand, and in this was laid a small roll of papyrus inscribed with the text of certain Chapters of the Book of the Dead, and thus the deceased was provided with additional security for the resurrection of his spiritual body in the world to come. The little rolls of papyrus are often inscribed with but short and fragmentary texts, but occasionally, as in the case of the priestess Anhai, a fine large papyrus, inscribed with numerous texts and illustrated with vignettes, was placed inside the figure of the god, who in this instance is in the form of Osiris only. It seems that the Ptah-Seker-Ausar figure was much used in the late period in Egypt, for many inscribed examples have been found which are not only illegible, but which prove that the artist had not the remotest idea of the meaning of the things which he was writing. It is possible that they were employed largely by the poor, among whom they seem to have served the purpose of the costly tomb.

Returning once more to the subject of wax figures, it may be wondered why such a very large proportion of the figures of the gods which were worn by the living and attached to the bodies of the dead as amulets are made of almost every kind of substance except wax. But the reason of this is not far to seek: wax is a substance which readily changes its form under heat and pressure, and it is also possible that the fact of its having been employed from time immemorial for making figures which were intended to work harm and not good to man, induced those who made amulets in the forms of the gods to select some other material. As a matter of fact, however, several figures of gods made of wax to serve as protective amulets are known, and a set of four, representing the four children of Horus, now preserved in the British Museum, are worthy of notice. The four children of Horus, or the gods of the four cardinal points, were called Mestha, Hâpi, Tuamutef, and Qebhsennuf, and with them were associated the goddesses Isis, Nephthys, Neith, and Serqet respectively. Mestha was man-headed, and represented the south, and protected the stomach and large intestines; Hâpi was dog-headed, and represented the north, and protected the small intestines; Tuamutef was jackal-headed and represented the east and protected the lungs and the heart; and Qebhsennuf was hawk-headed, and represented the west, and protected the liver and the gall-bladder. The various internal organs of men were removed from the body before it was mummified, and having been steeped in certain astringent substances and bitumen were wrapped up in bandages, and laid in four jars made of stone, marble, porcelain, earthenware, or wood. Each jar was placed under the protection of one of the four children of Horus, and as it was hollow, and its cover was made in the form of the head of the god who was represented by it, and as the jar by means of the inscription upon it became an abode of the god, it might well be said that the organ of the deceased which was put in it was actually placed inside the god. The custom of embalming the intestines separately is very old, and several examples of it in the XIth dynasty are known; even at that early period the four jars of mummified intestines were placed in a funeral chest, or coffer, which was mounted on a sledge, and drawn along in the funeral procession immediately after the coffin. In later times we find that many attempts were made to secure for the deceased the benefit of the protection of these four gods without incurring the expense of stone jars; this could be done by burying with him four models or "dummy" jars, or four porcelain figures of the four gods, or four wax ones. For some unknown reason the set referred to above was made of wax. The four children of Horus played a very important part in the funeral works of the early dynasties; they originally represented the four supports of heaven, but very soon each was regarded as the god of one of the four quarters of the earth, and also of that quarter of the heavens which was above it. As the constant prayer of the deceased was that he should be able to go about wherever he pleased, both on earth and in heaven, it was absolutely necessary for his welfare that he should propitiate these gods and place himself under their protection, which could only be secured by the recital of certain words of power over figures of them, or over jars made to represent them.

But of all the Egyptians who were skilled in working magic, Nectanebus, the last native king of Egypt, about B.C. 318, was the chief, if we may believe Greek tradition. According to Pseudo-Callisthenes, and the versions of his works which were translated into Pehlevi, Arabic, Syriac, and a score of other languages and dialects, this king was famous as a magician and a sage, and he was deeply learned in all the wisdom of the Egyptians. He knew what was in the depths of the Nile and of heaven, he was skilled in reading the stars, in interpreting omens, in casting nativities, in telling fortunes, and in predicting the future of the unborn child, and in working magic of every kind, as we shall see; he was said to be the lord of the earth, and to rule all kings by means of his magical powers. Whenever he was threatened with invasion by sea or by land he succeeded in destroying the power of his enemies, and in driving them from his coasts or frontiers; and this he did by the following means. If the enemy came against him by sea, instead of sending out his sailors to fight them, he retired into a certain chamber, and having brought forth a bowl which he kept for the purpose, he filled it with water, and then, having made wax figures of the ships and men of the enemy, and also of his own men and ships, he set them upon the water in the bowl, his men on one side, and those of the enemy on the other. He then came out, and having put on the cloak of an Egyptian prophet and taken an ebony rod in his hand, he returned into the chamber, and uttering words of power he invoked the gods who help men to work magic, and the winds, and the subterranean demons, which straightway came to his aid. By their means the figures of the men in wax sprang into life and began to fight, and the ships of wax began to move about likewise; but the figures which represented his own men vanquished those which represented the enemy, and as the figures of the ships and men of the hostile fleet sank through the water to the bottom of the bowl, even so did the real ships and men sink through the waters to the bottom of the sea. In this way he succeeded in maintaining his power, and he continued to occupy his kingdom in peace for a considerable period. But it fell out on a day that certain scouts came and informed Nectanebus that a multitude of the nations of the East had made a league together against Egypt, and that their allied forces were at that moment marching against him. When the king heard the news he laughed, and having said some scornful words about his enemies, he went into his private chamber, and pouring water into the bowl began to work magic in the usual way. But when he had spoken the words of power, he looked at the wax figures, and saw, to his dismay, that the gods of Egypt were steering the enemies' ships, and leading their soldiers to war against himself. Now as soon as Nectanebus saw this, he understood that the end of the kingdom of Egypt was at hand, for hitherto the gods had been wont to hold converse with him readily, and to lend him their help whenever he had need of it. He then quitted the chamber hastily, and having shaved off his hair and his beard, and disguised himself by putting on common apparel, be took ship and fled to Pella in Macedonia, where he established himself as a physician, and as an Egyptian soothsayer.

Omitting, for the present, any reference to the contents of the IVth chapter of Pseudo-Callisthenes, in which the casting of the nativity of Olympias by Nectanebus is described, we come to the passage in which the story of the way in which he sent a dream to the queen by means of a wax figure is told. His object was to persuade the queen that the Egyptian god Amen would come to her at night. To do this he left her presence, and going out into the desert he collected a number of herbs which he knew how to employ in causing people to dream dreams, and having brought them back with him be squeezed the juice out of them. He then made the figure of a woman in wax, and wrote upon it the name of Olympias, just as the priest of Thebes made the figure of Âpep in wax and cut his name upon it. Nectanebus then lit his lamp, and, having poured the juice of the herbs over the wax figure of the queen, he adjured the demons to such purpose that Olympias dreamed a dream in which the god Amen came to her and embraced her, and told her that she should give birth to a man-child who should avenge her on her husband Philip. But the means described above were not the only ones known to Nectanebus for procuring dreams, for when he wanted to make Philip of Macedon to see certain things in a dream, and to take a certain view about what he saw, he sent a hawk, which he had previously bewitched by magical words, to Philip as he lay asleep, and in a single night the hawk flew from Macedonia to the place where Philip was, and coming to him told him what things he should see in his dream, and he saw them. On the morrow Philip had the dream explained by an expounder of dreams, and he was satisfied that the child to whom his wife Olympias was about to give birth was the son of the god Amen (or Ammon) of Libya, who was regarded as the father of all the kings who ascended the throne of Egypt, who did not belong to the royal stock of that country.

Here, in connexion with the Egyptian use of wax figures, must be mentioned one or two stories and traditions of Alexander the Great which are, clearly, derived from Egyptian sources. The Arab writer, Abu-Shâker, who flourished in the XIIIth century of our era, mentions a tradition that Aristotle gave to Alexander a number of wax figures nailed down in a box, which was fastened by a chain, and which he ordered him never to let go out of his hand, or at least out of that of one of his confidential servants. The box was to go wherever Alexander went, and Aristotle taught him to recite certain formulae over it whenever he took it up or put it down. The figures in the box were intended to represent the various kinds of armed forces that Alexander was likely to find opposed to him. Some of the models held in their hands leaden swords which were curved backwards, and some had spears in their hands pointed head downwards, and some had bows with cut strings; all these were laid face downwards in the box. Viewed by what we know of the ideas which underlay the use of wax figures by the Egyptians and Greeks, it is clear that, in providing Alexander with these models and the words of power to use with them, Aristotle believed he was giving him the means of making his enemies to become like the figures in the box, and so they would be powerless to attack him.

In the Græco-Roman period wax figures were used in the performance of magical ceremonies of every kind, and the two following examples indicate that the ideas which underlay their use had not changed in the least. If a lover wished to secure the favours of his mistress, he is directed to make a figure of a dog in wax mixed with pitch, gum, etc., eight fingers long, and certain words of power are to be written over the place where his ribs should be. Next it was necessary to write on a tablet other words of power, or the names of beings who were supposed to possess magical powers; on this tablet the figure of the dog must be placed, and the tablet is made to rest upon a tripod. When this has been done the lover must recite the words of power which are written on the dog's side, and also the names which have been inscribed on the tablet, and one of two things will happen: *i.e.*, the dog will either snarl and snap at the lover, or he will bark. If he snarls and snaps the lover will not gain the object of his affections, but if he barks the lady will come to him. In the second example the lover is ordered to make two waxen figures; one in the form of Ares, and the other in the form of a woman. The female figure is to be in the posture of kneeling upon her knees with her hands tied behind her, and the male figure is to stand over her with his sword at her throat. On the limbs of the female figure a large number of the names of demons are to be written, and when this has been done, the lover must take thirteen bronze needles, and stick them in her limbs, saying as he does so, "I pierce" (here he mentions the name of the limb) "that she may think of me." The lover must next write certain words of power on a leaden plate, which must be tied to the wax figures with a string containing three hundred and sixty-five knots, and both figure and plate are to be buried in the grave of some one who has died young or who has been slain by violence. He must then recite a long incantation to the infernal gods, and if all these things be done in a proper manner the lover will obtain the woman's affections.

From Egypt, by way of Greece and Rome, the use of wax figures passed into Western Europe and England, and in the Middle Ages it found great favour with those who interested themselves in the working of the "black art," or who wished to do their neighbour or enemy an injury. Many stories are current of how in Italy and England ignorant or wicked-minded people made models of their enemies in wax and hung them up in the chimney, not too close to the fire, so that they might melt away slowly, and of how the people that were represented by such figures gradually lost the power over their limbs, and could not sleep, and slowly sickened and died. If pins and needles were stuck into the wax figures at stated times the sufferings of the living were made more agonizing, and their death much more painful.

Sharpe relates that about the end of the VIIth century king Duffus was so unpopular that "a company of hags roasted his image made of wax upon a wooden spit, reciting certain words of enchantment, and basting the figure with a poisonous liquor. These women when apprehended declared that as the wax melted, the body of the king should decay, and the words of enchantment prevented him from the refreshment of sleep." The two following extracts from Thomas Middleton's *The Witch* illustrate the views held about wax figures in England in the time of this writer.

I.

"*Heccat*. Is the heart of wax
Stuck full of magique needles?"
Stadlin. 'Tis done Heccat.
Heccat. And is the Farmer's picture, and his wive's,
Lay'd downe to th' fire yet?
Stadlin. They are a roasting both too.
Heccat. Good:
Then their marrowes are a melting subtelly
And three monethes sicknes sucks up life in 'em."

(Act i., scene 2.)

II.

"*Heccat*. What death is't you desire for Almachildes?
Duchesse. A sodaine and a subtle.
Heccat. Then I have fitted you.
Here lye the guifts of both; sodaine and subtle:
His picture made in wax, and gently molten
By a blew fire kindled with dead mens' eyes

Will waste him by degrees."

(Act v., scene 2)

Mr. Elworthy in his very interesting book "The Evil Eye" relates some striking examples of the burning of hearts stuck full of pins for magical purposes in recent years. Thus an old woman at Mendip had a pig that fell ill, and she at once made up her mind that the animal had been "overlooked"; in her trouble she consulted a "white witch," *i.e.* a "wise" man, and by his orders she acted thus. She obtained a sheep's heart, and having stuck it full of pins set it to roast before a fire, whilst her friends and neighbours sang:-

"It is not this heart I mean to burn.
But the person's heart I wish to turn,
Wishing them neither rest nor peace
Till they are dead and gone."

At intervals her son George sprinkled salt on the fire which added greatly to the weirdness of the scene, and at length, when the roasting had been continued until far into the night, a black cat jumped out from somewhere and was, of course, instantly declared to be the demon which had been exorcised. Again, in October, 1882, a heart stuck full of pins was found in a recess of a chimney in an old house in the village of Ashbrittle; and in 1890 another was found nailed up inside the "clavel" in the chimney of an old house at Staplegrove.

The art of making such figures King James I. attributes to the "Divell," and says in describing the things which witches are able to "effectuate by the power of their master. To some others at these times hee teacheth, how to make pictures of waxe or clay: That by the roasting thereof, the persons that they beare the name of, may be continually melted or dried away by continuall sicknesse... They can bewitch and take the life of men or women, by roasting of the pictures, as I spake of before, which likewise is verie possible to their Maister to performe, for although (as I said before) that instrument of waxe have no vertue in that turne doing, yet may hee not very well, even by the same measure that his conjured slaves, melts that waxe at the fire, may hee not, I say at these same times, subtily, as a sprite, so weaken and scatter the spirites of life of the patient, as may make him on the one part, for faintnesse, so sweate it out the humour of his bodie: And on the other parte, for the not concurrence of these spirites, which causes his digestion, so debilitate his stomacke, that this humour radicall continually sweating out on the one part, and no new good sucke being put in the place thereof, for lacke of digestion on the other, he at last shall vanish away, even as his picture will die at the fire? And that knavish and cunning workeman, by troubling him, onely at sometimes, makes a proportion, so neere betwixt the working of the one and the other, that both shall end as it were at one time."

Thus we have seen that the belief in the efficacy of wax figures is at least six thousand years old, and judging from passages in the works of modern writers its existence is not unknown in our own country at the present time.

This chapter may be fittingly ended by a notice of the benefits which accrued to a Christian merchant in the Levant from the use of a wax figure. According to an Ethiopic manuscript in the British Museum this man was a shipowner as well as a merchant, and be was wont to send his goods to market in his own ships; in his day, however, the sea was infested with pirates, and he lost greatly through their successful attacks upon his vessels. At length he determined to travel in one of his own ships with a number of armed men, so that he might be able to resist any attack which the pirates might make, and punish them for their robberies in times past. Soon after he had sailed he fell in with a pirate vessel, and a fight at once took place between his crew and the robbers, in the course of which he was shot in the eye by an arrow; he stopped the combat and then sailed for a port which was situated near a monastery, wherein the Virgin Mary was reported to work miracles by means of a picture of herself which was hung up in it. When the merchant arrived in port he was so ill through the wound in his eye that he could not be moved, and it was found that a portion of the arrow which had struck him remained embedded in it; and unless he could obtain the Virgin's help speedily he felt that his death was nigh. In this difficulty a certain Christian came to the ship and made a wax figure of the merchant, and, having stuck in one eye a model of the arrow which had struck him, carried the figure to the monastery, which was some miles off, and caused the monks to allow him to bring it nigh to the picture of the Virgin. When this had been done, and prayers had been made to her, the figure of the Virgin stretched out its hand, and straightway pulled the model of the arrow out of the eye of the wax figure of the merchant in such a way that no broken fragment remained behind. When the wax figure had been taken back to the ship, it was found that the piece of broken arrow had been extracted from the merchant's eye at the very moment when the Virgin had drawn out the arrow from the eye of the wax figure. The merchant's eye then healed, and he recovered his sight.

CHAPTER IV

MAGICAL PICTURES AND FORMULAE, SPELLS, ETC.

FROM what has been said above it is clear that the Egyptian believed it possible to vivify by means of formulae and words of power any figure made in the form of a man or animal, and to make it work either on behalf of or against his fellow man. Besides this, he believed greatly in the efficacy of representations or pictures of the gods, and of divine beings and things, provided that words of power properly recited by properly appointed people were recited over them. If this fact be borne in mind a great many difficulties in understanding religious texts disappear, and many apparently childish facts are seen to have an important meaning. If we look into the tombs of the early period we see painted on the walls numbers of scenes in which the deceased is represented making offerings to the gods and performing religious ceremonies, as well as numbers of others in which he is directing the work of his estate and ruling his household. It was not altogether the result of pride that such pictures were painted on the walls of tombs, for at the bottom of his heart the Egyptian hoped and believed that they were in reality representations of what he would do in the next world, and he trusted that the words of his prayers would turn pictures into realities, and drawings into substances. The wealthy Egyptian left behind him the means for making the offerings which his *ka*, or double, needed, and was able to provide for the maintenance of his tomb and of the *ka* chapel and of the priest or priests who ministered to it. It was an article of faith among all classes that unless the *ka* was properly fed it would be driven to wander about and pick up filth and anything else of that nature which it found in its path, as we may see from the LIInd Chapter of the Book of the Dead, in which the deceased says, "That which is an abomination unto me, that which is an abomination unto me let me not eat. That which is an abomination unto me, that which is an abomination unto me is filth; let me not eat of it instead of the cakes [which are offered unto] the Doubles (*kau*). Let it not light upon my body; let me not be obliged to take it into my hands; and let me not be obliged to walk thereon in my sandals." And in the CLXXXIXth Chapter he prays that he may not be obliged to drink filthy water or be defiled in any way by it. The rich man, even, was not certain that the appointed offerings of meat and drink could or would be made in his tomb in perpetuity: what then was the poor man to do to save his *ka* from the ignominy of eating filth and drinking dirty water? To get out of this difficulty the model of an altar in stone was made, and models of cakes, vases of water, fruit, meat, etc., were placed upon it; in cases where this was not possible figures of the offerings were sculptured upon the stone itself; in others, where even the expense of an altar could not be borne by the relatives of the dead, an altar with offerings painted upon it was placed in the tomb, and as long as it existed through the prayers recited, the *ka* did not lack food. Sometimes neither altar, nor model nor picture of an altar was placed in the tomb, and the prayer that sepulchral meals might be given to the deceased by the gods, which was inscribed upon some article of funeral furniture, was the only provision made for the wants of the *ka*; but every time any one who passed by the tomb recited that prayer, and coupled with it the name of the man who was buried in it, his *ka* was provided with a fresh supply of meat and drink offerings, for the models or pictures of them in the inscription straightway became veritable substances. On the insides of the wooden coffins of the XIIth dynasty, about B.C. 2500, are painted whole series of objects which, in still earlier times, were actually placed in the tombs with the mummy; but little by little men ceased to provide the numerous articles connected with the sepulture of the dead which the old ritual prescribed, and they trusted to the texts and formulae which they painted on the coffin to turn pictures into substances, and besides the pillow they placed little else in the tomb.

About a thousand years later, when the religious texts which formed the Book of the Dead were written upon papyri instead of coffins, a large number of illustrations or vignettes were added to them; to many of these special importance was attached, and the following are worthy of note.

It will be remembered that the CXXVth Chapter of the Book of the Dead contains the so-called "Negative Confession" which is recited in the Hall of Maâti, and a number of names of gods and beings, the knowledge of which is most important for the welfare of the deceased. At the end of the Chapter we find the following statement:-

"This chapter shall be said by the deceased after he hath been cleansed and purified, and when he is arrayed in apparel, and is shod with white leather sandals, and his eyes have been painted with antimony, and his body hath been anointed with *ânti* unguent, and when he hath made offerings of oxen, and birds, and incense, and cakes, and ale, and garden herbs. And behold, thou shalt paint a picture of what shall happen in the Hall of Maâti upon a new tile moulded from earth, upon which neither a pig nor any other animal hath trodden. And if thou writest upon it this chapter the deceased shall flourish; and his children shall flourish; and his name shall never fall into oblivion; and bread, and cakes, and sweetmeats, and wine, and meat shall be given unto him at the altar of the great god; and he shall not be turned back at any door in the underworld; and he shall be brought in along with the Kings of the North and South; and he shall be in the following of Osiris always and for ever." Here, then, we have an excellent example of the far-reaching effects of a picture accompanied by the proper words of power, and every picture in the Book of the Dead was equally efficacious in producing a certain result, that result being always connected with the welfare of the dead.

According to several passages and chapters the deceased was terrified lest he should lack both air and water, as well as food, in the underworld, and, to do away with all risk of such a calamity happening, pictures, in which he is represented holding a sail (the symbol of air and wind and breath) in his hands, and standing up to his ankles in water, were painted on his papyrus, and texts similar to the following were written below them. "My mouth and my nostrils are opened in Tattu (Busiris), and I have my place of peace in Annu (Heliopolis) which is my house; it was built for me by the goddess Sesheta, and the god Khnemu set it upon its walls for me...." "Hail, thou god Tem, grant thou unto me the sweet breath which dwelleth in thy nostrils! I embrace the great throne which is in Khemennu (Hermopolis), and I keep watch over the Egg of the Great Cackler; I germinate as it germinateth; I live as it liveth; and my breath is its breath." But yet another "exceeding great mystery" had to be performed if the deceased was to be enabled to enter into heaven by its four doors at will, and to enjoy the air which came through each. The north wind belonged to Osiris, the south wind to Râ, the west wind to Isis, and the east wind to Nephthys; and for the deceased to obtain power over each and all of these it was necessary for him to be master of the doors through which they blew. This power could only be obtained by causing pictures of the four doors to be painted on the coffin with a figure of Thoth opening each. Some special importance was attached to these, for the rubric says, "Let none who is outside know this chapter, for it is a great mystery, and those who dwell in the swamps (*i.e.*, the ignorant) know it not. Thou shalt not do this in the presence of any person except thy father, or thy son, or thyself alone; for it is indeed an exceedingly great mystery which no man whatever knoweth."

One of the delights coveted by the deceased was to sail over heaven in the boat of Râ, in company with the gods of the funeral cycle of Osiris; this happiness could be secured for him by painting certain pictures, and by saying over them certain words of power. On a piece of clean papyrus a boat is to be drawn with ink made of green *âbut* mixed with *ânti* water, and in it are to be figures of Isis, Thoth, Shu, and Khepera, and the deceased; when this has been done the papyrus must be fastened to the breast of the deceased, care being taken that it does not actually touch his body. Then shall his spirit enter into the boat of Râ each day, and the god Thoth shall take heed to him, and he shall sail about with Râ into any place that he wisheth. Elsewhere it is ordered that the boat of Râ be painted "in a pure place," and in the bows is to be painted a figure of the deceased; but Râ was supposed to travel in one boat (called "Âtet") until noon, and another (called "Sektet") until sunset, and provision had to be made for the deceased in both boats. How was this to be done? On one side of the picture of the boat a figure of the morning boat of Râ was to be drawn, and on the other a figure of the afternoon boat; thus the one picture was capable of becoming two boats. And, provided the proper offerings were made for the deceased on the birthday of Osiris, his soul would live for ever, and he would not die a second time. According to the rubric to the chapter in which these directions are given, the text of it is as old, at least, as the time of Hesepti, the fifth king of the Ist dynasty, who reigned about B.C. 4350, and the custom of painting the boat upon papyrus is probably contemporaneous. The two following rubrics from Chapters CXXXIII. and CXXXIV., respectively, will explain still further the importance of such pictures:-

1. *"This chapter shall be recited over a boat four cubits in length, and made of green porcelain [on which have been painted] the divine sovereign chiefs of the cities; and a figure of heaven with its stars shall be made also, and this thou shalt have made ceremonially pure by means of natron and incense. And behold, thou shalt make an image of Râ in yellow colour upon a new plaque and set it at the bows of the boat. And behold, thou shalt make an image of the spirit which thou dost wish to make perfect [and place it] in this boat, and thou shalt make it to travel about in the boat [which. shall be made in the form of the boat] of Râ; and he shall see the form of the god Râ himself therein. Let not the eye of any man whatsoever look upon it, with the exception of thine own self,*

or thy father, or thy son, and guard [this] with great care. Then shall the spirit be perfect in the heart of Râ, and it shall give unto him power with the company of the gods; and the gods shall look upon him as a divine being like unto themselves; and mankind and the dead shall fall down upon their faces, and he shall be seen in the underworld in the form of the radiance of Râ."

2. *"This chapter shall be recited over a hawk standing and having the white crown upon his head, [and over figures of] the gods Tem, Shu, Tefnut, Seb, Nut, Osiris, Isis, Suti, and Nephthys, painted in yellow colour upon a new plaque, which shall be placed in [a model of] the boat [of Râ], along with a figure of the spirit whom thou wouldst make perfect, These thou shalt anoint with cedar oil, and incense shall be offered up to them on the fire, and feathered fowl, shall be roasted. It is an act of praise to Râ as he journeyeth, and it shall cause a man to have his being along with Râ day by day, whithersoever the god voyageth; and it shall destroy the enemies of Râ in very truth regularly and continually."*

Many of the pictures or vignettes carry their own interpretations with them, *e.g.*, the picture of the soul hovering
over the dead body which lies beneath it on the bier at once
suggests the reunion of the soul with the body; the picture
of the deceased walking away from a "block of slaughter"
and a knife dripping with blood suggests escape from a
cruel death; the picture of a soul and spirit standing before
an open door suggests that the soul has freedom to wander
about at will; and the picture of the soul and the shadow
in the act of passing out through the door of the tomb
indicates clearly that these parts of man's economy are not
shut up in the tomb for all eternity. But the ideas which
prompted the painting of other vignettes are not so clear,
e.g., those which accompany Chapters CLXII.-CLXV.
in the late or Säite Recension of the Book of the Dead,
although, fortunately, the rubrics to these chapters make
their object clear. Thus the picture which stands above
Chapter CLXII. is that of a cow having upon her head
horns, a disk, and two plumes, and from the rubric we
learn that a figure of it was to be made in gold and fastened
to the neck of the deceased, and that another, drawn upon
new papyrus, was to be placed under his head. If this be
done "then shall abundant warmth be in him throughout,
even like that which was in him when he was upon earth.
And he shall become like a god in the underworld, and he

shall never be turned back at any of the gates thereof." The words of the chapter have great protective power (*i.e.*, are a charm of the greatest importance) we are told, "for it was made by the cow for her son Râ when he was setting, and when his habitation was surrounded by a company of beings of fire." Now the cow is, of course, Isis-Hathor, and both the words and the picture refer to some event in the life of Râ, or Horus. It is quite evident that the words of power, or charm, uttered by Isis-Hathor delivered the god out of some trouble, and the idea is that as it delivered the god, and was of benefit to him, even so will it deliver the deceased and be of benefit to him. The words of power read:- "O Amen, O Amen, who art in heaven, turn thy face upon the dead body of thy son, and make him sound and strong in the underworld." And again we are warned that the words are "a great mystery" and that "the eye of no man whatsoever must see it, for it is a thing of abomination for [every man] to know it. Hide it, therefore; the Book of the lady of the hidden temple is its name."

An examination of mummies of the late period shews that the Egyptians did actually draw a figure of the cow upon papyrus and lay it under the head of the deceased, and that the cow is only one figure among a number of others which were drawn on the same papyrus. With the figures magical texts were inscribed and in course of time, when the papyrus had been mounted upon linen, it superseded the gold figure of the cow which was fastened to the neck of the deceased, and became, strictly speaking an amulet, though its usual name among archaeologists is "hypocephalus." It will be noticed that the hypocephalus is round; this is due to the fact that it represents the pupil of the Eye of Horus, which from time immemorial in Egypt was regarded as the source of all generative power, and of reproduction and life. The first group of gods are:- Nehebka offering to Horus his Eye, a goddess with the Eye of Horus for a head, the cow of Isis-Hathor described above, the four children of Horus, two lions, a member of the human body, the pylon of heads of Khnemu the god of reproduction, and Horus-Râ. In the second are the boat of the Sun being poled along by Horus, and the boat of the Moon, with Harpocrates in the bow. In the other scenes we have the god Khepera in his boat, Horus in his boat, and Horus-Sept in his boat. The god with two faces represents the double aspect of the sun in setting and rising, and the god with the rams' heads, who is being adored by apes, is a mystical form of Khnemu, one of the great gods of reproduction, who in still later times became the being whose name under the form of Khnumis or Khnoubis occupied such an important position among the magical names which were in use among the Gnostics. The two following prayers from the hypocephalus will illustrate the words of power addressed to Amen, *i.e.*, the Hidden One, quoted above:- 1. "I am the Hidden One in the hidden place. I am a perfect spirit among the companions of Râ, and I have gone in and come forth among the perfect souls. I am the mighty Soul of saffron-coloured form. I have come forth from the underworld at pleasure. I have come. I have come forth from the Eye of Horus. I have come forth from the underworld with Râ from the House of the Great Aged One in Heliopolis. I am one of the spirits who come forth from the underworld: grant thou unto me the things which my body needeth, and heaven for my soul, and a hidden place for my mummy." 2. "May the god, who himself is hidden, and whose face is concealed, who shineth upon the world in his forms of existence, and in the underworld, grant that my soul may live for ever! May the great god in his disk give his rays in the underworld of Heliopolis! Grant thou unto me an entrance and an exit in the underworld without let or hindrance."

Chapter CLXIII. of the Book of the Dead was written to prevent the body of a man mouldering away in the underworld, and to deliver him from the souls which were so unfortunate as to be shut in the various places thereof, but in order to make it thoroughly efficacious it was ordered to be recited over three pictures: (1) a serpent with legs, having a disk and two horns upon its head; (2) an *utchat*, or Eye of Horus, "in the pupil of which shall be a figure of the God of the lifted hand with the face of a divine soul, and having plumes and a back like a hawk"; (3) an *utchat*, or Eye of Horus, "in the pupil of which there shall be a figure of the God of the lifted hand with the face of the goddess Neith, and having plumes and a back like a hawk." If these things be done for the deceased "he shall not be turned back at any gate of the underworld, he shall eat, and drink, and perform the natural functions of his body as he did when he was upon earth; and none shall rise up to cry out against him; and he shall be protected from the hands of the enemy for ever and ever."

The words of power which form the CLXIVth Chapter to be effectual had to be recited over a figure of the goddess Mut which was to have three heads. The first head was like that of the goddess Pekhat and had plumes; the second was like that of a man and had upon it the crowns of the South and North; the third was like that of a vulture and had upon it plumes; the figure had a pair of wings, and the claws of a lion. This figure was painted in black, green, and yellow colours upon a piece of *anes* linen; in front of it and behind it was painted a dwarf who wore plumes upon his head. One hand and arm of each dwarf were raised, and each had two faces, one being that of a hawk and the other that of a man; the body of each was fat. These figures having been made, we are told that the deceased shall be "like unto a god with the gods of the underworld; he shall never, never be turned back; his flesh and his bones shall be like those of one who hath never been dead; he shall drink water at the source of the stream; a homestead shall be given unto him in Sekhet-Aaru; he shall become a star of heaven; he shall set out to do battle with the serpent fiend Nekau and with Tar, who are in the underworld; he shall not be shut in along with the souls which are fettered; he shall have power to deliver himself wherever he may be; and worms shall not devour him."

Again, the words of power which form the CLXVth Chapter to be effectual were ordered by the rubric to "be recited over a figure of the God of the lifted hand, which shall have plumes upon its head; the legs thereof shall be wide apart, and the middle portion of it shall be in the form of a beetle, and it shall be painted blue with a paint made of lapis-lazuli mixed with *qamai* water. And it shall be recited over a figure with a head like unto that of a man, and the hands and the arms thereof shall be stretched away from his body; above its right shoulder shall there be the head of a ram, and above its left shoulder shall there be the head of a ram. And thou shalt paint the figure of the God of the lifted hand upon a piece of linen immediately over the heart of the deceased, and thou shalt paint the other over his breast; but let not the god Sukati who is in the underworld know it." If these things be done, "the deceased shall drink water from the source of the stream, and he shall shine like the stars in the heavens above." It is probable that Chapters CLXIL-CLXV. were composed at a comparatively late date.

Yet another example of the magical pictures of the Book of the Dead must here be given. The vignette of Chapter CXLVIII. contains pictures of seven cows "and their bull," and of four rudders; the seven cows have reference to the seven Hathor goddesses, the bull is, of course, a form of Râ, and the four rudders refer to the four quarters of the earth and to the four cardinal points. The text of the Chapter contains the names of the cows and of the bull, and of the rudders, and certain prayers for sepulchral offerings. Now the deceased would be provided with "abundance of food regularly and continually for ever," if the following things were done for him. Figures of the cows and of their bull and of the rudders were to be painted in colours upon a board (?), and when Râ, the Sun-god, rose upon them the friends of the deceased were to place offerings before them; these offerings would be received mystically by the gods and goddesses whom the figures represented, and in return they would bestow upon the deceased all the offerings or gifts of meat and drink which he would require. Moreover, "if this be done," we are told, "Râ shall be a rudder for the deceased, and he shall be a strength protecting him, and he shall make an end of all his enemies for him in the underworld, and in heaven, and upon earth, and in every place wherever he may enter."

We have seen above, in the description of the amulets which the Egyptians used, how both the substance of the amulet and the words which were inscribed upon it possessed magical powers, but we may learn from several instances given in the papyri that the written words alone were sufficient in some cases to produce remarkable effects. This is, of course, a very natural development, and charms or words of power which needed nothing but to be written on papyrus or linen to produce a magical effect would be popular with all classes of men and women, and especially among the poor and the ignorant. The written word has been regarded in the East with reverence from time immemorial, and a copy of a sacred writing or text is worn or carried about to this day with much the same ideas and beliefs about its power to protect as in the earliest times. In ancient Egypt the whole Book of the Dead, as well as the various sections of it which are usually copied on papyri, consisted of a series of "words of power," and the modern Egyptian looks upon the Koran in the same light as his ancestor looked upon the older work. A curious passage in the text inscribed on the inside of the pyramid of Unas reads (1. 583), "The bone and flesh which possess no writing are wretched, but, behold, the writing of Unas is under the great seal, and behold, it is not under the little seal." It is difficult to explain the passage fully, but there is no doubt that we have here an allusion to the custom of placing writings believed to be possessed of magical powers with the dead. Certain passages or sections of the religious books of ancient nations have always been held to be of more importance than others, and considering the great length of such compositions this is not to be wondered at. Among the Egyptians two forms of the LXIVth Chapter of the Book of the Dead were in use, and there is no doubt whatever that the shorter form, as far back as the Ist dynasty, about B.C. 4300, was intended to be a summary of the whole work, and that the recital of it was held to be as efficacious as the recital of all the rest of it. It is a remarkable fact that this form is called "The Chapter of knowing the 'Chapters of Coming Forth by Day' in a single Chapter," and that it is declared to date from the time of Hesepti, a king of the Ist dynasty, about B.C. 4300, whilst the "finding" of the longer form is attributed to the reign of Men-kau-Râ (Mycerinus), a king of the IVth dynasty, about B.C. 3600. It is interesting to note how persistently certain chapters and formulae occur in funeral papyri of different periods, and the explanation seems to be that a popular selection was made at an early date, and that this selection was copied with such additions or omissions as the means of the friends of the deceased allowed or made necessary. One thing is quite certain: every man in Egypt died in the firm belief that in the course of his journey into the next world he would be provided with words of power which would enable him to make his way thither unhindered, and give him abundance of meat and drink. We may see this view which was held concerning words of power from the following passages:- "May Thoth, who is filled and furnished with words of power, come and loose the bandages, even the bandages of Set which fetter my mouth... . Now as concerning the words of power and all the words which may be spoken against me, may the gods resist them, and may each and every one of the company of the gods withstand them." "Behold, I gather together the word of power from wherever it is, and from any person with whom it is, swifter than greyhounds and quicker than light." To the crocodile which cometh to carry off from the deceased his words of power he says, "Get thee back, return, get thee back, thou crocodile fiend Sui! Thou shalt not advance to me, for I live by reason of the words of power which I have with me... . Heaven hath power over its seasons, and the words of power have dominion over that which they possess; my mouth therefore shall have power over the words of power which are therein." "I am clothed (?) and am wholly provided with thy magical words, O Râ, the which are in the heaven above me, and in the earth beneath Me." To the two Sister-Mert goddesses the deceased says, "My message to you is my words of power. I shine from the Sektet boat, I am Horus the son of Isis, and I have come to see my father Osiris." "I have become a spirit in my forms, I have gained the mastery over my words of power, and it is decreed for me to be a spirit." "Hail, thou that cuttest off heads, and slittest brows, thou who puttest away the memory of evil things from the mouth of the spirits by means of the words of power which they have within them, ... let not my mouth be shut fast by reason of the words of power which thou hast within thee.... Get thee back, and depart before the words which the goddess Isis uttered when thou didst come to cast the recollection of evil things into the mouth of Osiris." On the amulet of the Buckle we have inscribed the words, "May the blood of Isis, and the powers of Isis, and the words of power of Isis be mighty to protect this mighty one," etc., and in the address which Thoth makes to Osiris he says, "I am Thoth, the favoured one of Râ, the lord of might, who bringeth to a prosperous end that which he doeth, the mighty one of words of power, who is in the boat of millions of years, the lord of laws, the subduer of the two lands," etc.

From the above passages we not only learn how great was the confidence which the deceased placed in his words of power, but also that the sources from which they sprang were the gods Thoth and Isis. It will be remembered that Thoth is called the "scribe of the gods," the "lord of writing," the "master of papyrus," the maker of the palette and the ink-jar," the "lord of divine words," *i.e.*, the holy writings or scriptures, and as he was the lord of books and master of the power of speech, he was considered to be the possessor of all knowledge both human and divine. At the creation of the world it was he who reduced to words the will of the unseen and unknown creative Power, and who uttered them in such wise that the universe came into being, and it was he who proved himself by the exercise of his knowledge to be the protector and friend of Osiris, and of Isis, and of their son Horus. From the evidence of the texts we know that it was not by physical might that Thoth helped these three gods, but by giving them words of power and instructing them how to use them. We know that Osiris vanquished his foes, and that he reconstituted his body, and became the king of the underworld and god of the dead, but he was only able to do these things by means of the words of power which Thoth had given to him, and which he had taught him to pronounce properly and in a proper tone of voice. It is this belief which makes the deceased cry out, "Hail, Thoth, who madest Osiris victorious over his enemies, make thou Ani to be victorious over his enemies in the presence of the great and sovereign princes who are in Tattu," or in any other place. Without the words of power given to him by Thoth, Osiris would have been powerless under the attacks of his foes, and similarly the dead man, who was always identified with Osiris, would have passed out of existence at his death but for the words of power provided by the writings that were buried with him. In the Judgment Scene it is Thoth who reports to the gods the result of the weighing of the heart in the balance, and who has supplied its owner with the words which he has uttered in his supplications, and whatever can be said in favour of the deceased he says to the gods, and whatever can be done for him he does. But apart from being the protector and friend of Osiris, Thoth was the refuge to which Isis fled in her trouble. The words of a hymn declare that she knew "how to turn aside evil hap," and that she was "strong of tongue, and uttered the words of power which she knew with correct pronunciation, and halted not in her speech, and was perfect both in giving the command and in saying the word," but this description only proves that she had been instructed by Thoth in the art of uttering words of power with effect, and to him, indeed, she owed more than this. When she found the dead body of her husband Osiris, she hovered about over it in the form of a bird, making air by the beating of her wings, and sending forth light from the sheen of her feathers, and at length she roused the dead to life by her words of power; as the result of the embrace which followed this meeting Horus was born, and his mother suckled him and tended him in her hiding-place in the papyrus swamps. After a time she was persecuted by Set, her husband's murderer, who, it seems, shut her and her son Horus up in a house as prisoners. Owing, however, to the help which Thoth gave her, she came forth by night and was accompanied on her journey by seven scorpions, called respectively Tefen, Befen, Mestet, Mestetef, Petet, Thetet, and Matet, the last three of which pointed out the way.

The guide of the way brought her to the swamps of Persui, and to the town of the two goddesses of the sandals where the swampy country of Athu begins. Journeying on they came to Teb, where the chief of the district had a house for his ladies; now the mistress of the house would not admit Isis on account of the scorpions that were with her, for she had looked out of her door and watched Isis coming. On this the scorpions took counsel together and wished to sting her by means of the scorpion Tefen, but at this moment a poor woman who lived in the marshes opened the door of her cottage to Isis, and the goddess took shelter therein. Meanwhile the scorpion had crept under the door into the house of the governor, and stung the son of the lady of the house, and also set the place on fire; no water could quench the fire, and there was no rain to do it, for it was not then the rainy season. Now these things happened to the woman who had done no active harm to Isis, and the poor creature wandered about the streets of the city uttering loud cries of grief and distress because she knew not whether her boy would live or die.

When Isis saw this she was sorry for the child who had been stung, and as he was blameless in the matter of the door of his mother's house being shut in the face of the goddess, she determined to save him. Thereupon she cried out to the distraught mother, saying, "Come to me, come to me! For my word is a talisman which beareth life. I am a daughter well known in thy city also, and I will do away the evil by means of the word of my mouth which my father hath taught me, for I am the daughter of his own body." Then Isis laid her hands upon the body of the boy, and in order to bring back the spirit into his body said-

"Come Tefen, appear upon the ground, depart hence, come not nigh!

*"Come poison of Befen, appear upon the ground.
I am Isis, the goddess, the lady of words of power,
who doeth deeds of magic, the words of whose
voice are charms.*

*"Obey me, O every reptile that stingeth, and fall
down headlong!*

*"O poison of [Mestet and] Mestetef, mount not
upwards!*

*"O poison of Petet and Thetet, draw not nigh! O
Matet, fall down headlong!"*

The goddess Isis then uttered certain words of the charm which had been given to her by the god Seb in order to keep poison away from her, and said, "Turn away, get away, retreat, O poison," adding the words "Mer-Râ" in the morning and "The Egg of the Goose appeareth from out of the sycamore" in the evening, as she turned to the scorpions. Both these sentences were talismans. After this Isis lamented that she was more lonely and wretched than all the people of Egypt, and that she had become like an old man who hath ceased to look upon and to visit fair women in their houses; and she ordered the scorpions to turn away their looks from her and to show her the way to the marshes and to the secret place which is in the city of Khebt. Then the words of the cry, "The boy liveth, the poison dieth! As the sun liveth, so the poison dieth," were uttered, and the fire in the house of the woman was extinguished, and heaven rejoiced at the words of Isis. When Isis had said that the "son of the woman had been stung because his mother had shut the door of her house in her face, and had done nothing for her," the words of the cry, "The boy liveth and the poison dieth," were again uttered, and the son of the woman recovered.

Isis then continues her narrative thus:-"I Isis conceived a child, and was great with child of Horus. I, a goddess, gave birth to Horus, the son of Isis, upon an island (or nest) in Athu the region of swamps; and I rejoiced greatly because of this, for I regarded Horus as a gift which would repay me for the loss of his father. I hid him most carefully and concealed him in my anxiety, and indeed he was well hidden, and then I went away to the city of Am. When I had saluted the inhabitants thereof I turned back to seek the child, so that I might give him suck and take him in my arms again. But I found my sucking-child Horus the fair golden one, well nigh dead! He had bedewed the ground with the water from his eye and with the foam from his lips, his body was stiff, his heart was still, and no muscle in any of his limbs moved. Then I uttered a bitter cry of grief, and the dwellers in the papyrus swamps ran to me straightway from out of their houses, and they bewailed the greatness of my calamity; but none of them opened his mouth to speak, for every one was in deep sorrow for me, and no man knew how to bring back life into Horus. Then there came to me a certain woman who was well known in her city, for she belonged to a noble family, and she tried to rekindle the life in Horus, but although her heart was full of her knowledge my son remained motionless." Meanwhile the folk remarked that the son of the divine mother Isis had been protected against his brother Set, that the plants among which he had been hidden could not be penetrated by any hostile being, that the words of power of Temu, the father of the gods, "who is in heaven," should have preserved the life of Horus, that Set his brother could not possibly have had access to where the child was, who, in any case, had been protected against his wickedness; and at length it was discovered that Horus had been stung by a scorpion, and that the reptile "which destroyeth the heart" had wounded him, and had probably killed him.

At this juncture Nephthys arrived, and went round about among the papyrus swamps weeping bitterly because of the affliction of her sister Isis; with her also was Serqet, the goddess of scorpions, who asked continually, "What hath happened to the child Horus?" Then Nephthys said to Isis, "Cry out in prayer unto heaven, and let the mariners in the boat of Râ cease to row, and let not the boat of Râ move further on its course for the sake of the child Horus"; and forthwith Isis sent forth her cry up to heaven, and made her request come unto the "Boat of millions of years," and the Sun stood still and his boat moved not from its place by reason of the goddess's petition. Out from the boat came the god Thoth provided with magical powers, and bearing with him the great power to command in such wise that the words of his mouth must be fulfilled straightway; and he spake to Isis, saying "O thou goddess Isis, whose mouth knoweth how to utter charms (*or* talismans), no suffering shall come upon thy child Horus, for his health and safety depend upon the boat of Râ. I have come this day in the divine boat of the Disk (Aten) to the place where it was yesterday. When darkness (or night) ruleth, the light shall vanquish it for the health (*or* safety) of Horus for the sake ōf his mother Isis and similarly shall it happen unto every one who possesseth what is [here] written(?)." What took place next is, of course, evident. The child Horus was restored to life, to the great joy of his mother Isis, who was more indebted than ever to the god Thoth for coming to deliver her out of her trouble on the death of her son, just as he had done on the death of her husband. Now because

Isis had revivified both her husband and her son by the words of power and talismans which she possessed, mortal man thought it was absolutely necessary for him to secure her favour and protection at any cost, for eternal life and death were in her hands. As time went on the Egyptians revered her more and more, and as she was the lady of the gods and of heaven, power equal to that possessed by Râ himself was ascribed to her. Indeed, according to a legend which has come down to us, and which written upon papyrus or linen formed a magical formula against the poison of reptiles of all kinds, she made a bold attempt to wrest the power of Râ from him and to make herself mistress of the universe. The way in which she did this is told in a hieratic papyrus preserved at Turin, from which the following rendering has been made; the merit of first discovering the correct meaning of the text belongs to M. Lefébure.

THE LEGEND OF RÂ AND ISIS.

"The Chapter of the divine god, the self-created being who made the heavens and the earth, and the winds [which give] life, and the fire, and the gods, and men, and beasts, and cattle, and reptiles, and the fowl of the air and the fish of the sea; he is the king of men and of gods, he hath one period of life (?) and with him periods of one hundred and twenty years each are but as years; his names are manifold and unknown, the gods even know them not.

"Now Isis was a woman who possessed words of power; her heart was wearied with the millions of men, therefore she chose the millions of the gods, but she esteemed more highly the millions of the spirits (*khu*). And she meditated in her heart, saying, 'Cannot I by means of the sacred name of God make myself mistress of the earth and become a goddess like unto Râ in heaven and upon earth?' Now behold, each day Râ entered at the head of his holy mariners and established himself upon the throne of the two horizons. Now the divine one (*i.e.*, Râ) had grown old, he dribbled at the mouth, his spittle fell upon the earth, and his slobbering dropped upon the ground. And Isis kneaded it with earth in her hand, and formed thereof a sacred serpent in the form of a dart; she did not set it upright before her face, but let it lie upon the ground in the path whereby the great god went forth, according to his hearts desire, into his double kingdom. Now the holy god arose, and the gods who followed him as though he were Pharaoh went with him; and he came forth according to his daily wont; and the sacred serpent bit him. The flame of life departed from him, and he who dwelt among the cedars (?) was overcome. The holy god opened his mouth, and the cry of his majesty reached unto heaven; his company of gods said, 'What hath happened?' and his gods exclaimed, 'What is it?' But Râ could not answer, for his jaws trembled and all his members quaked; the poison spread swiftly through his flesh just as the Nile rusheth through all his land. When the great god had stablished his heart, he cried unto those who were in his train, saying, 'Come unto me, O ye who have come into being from my body, ye gods who have come forth from me, make ye known unto Khepera that a dire calamity hath fallen upon me. My heart perceiveth it, but my eyes see it not; my hand hath not caused it, nor do I know who hath done this unto me. Never have I felt such pain, neither can sickness cause more woe than this. I am a prince, the son of a prince, the sacred essence which hath proceeded from God. I am the great one, the son of the great one, and my father planned my name; I have multitudes of names and multitudes of forms, and my being is in every god. I have been proclaimed by the heralds Temu and Horus, and my father and my mother uttered my name; but it hath been hidden within me by him that begat me, who would not that the words of power of any seer should have dominion over me. I came forth to look upon that which I had made, I was passing through the world which I had created, when lo! something stung me, but what I know not. Is it fire? Is it water? My heart is on fire, my flesh quaketh, and trembling hath seized all my limbs. Let there be brought unto me my children, the gods, who possess the words of power and magical speech, and mouths which know how to utter them, and also powers which reach even unto the heavens. Then the children of every god came unto him uttering cries of grief. And Isis also came, bringing with her her words of magical power, and her mouth was full of the breath of life; for her talismans vanquish the pains of sickness, and her words make to live again the throats of those who are dead. And she spake, saying, 'What hath come to pass, O holy Father? What hath happened? Is it that a serpent hath bitten thee, and that a thing which thou hast created hath lifted up his head against thee? Verily it shall be cast down by my effective words of power, and I will drive it away from before the sight of thy sunbeams.' The holy god opened his mouth and said, I was passing along my path, and I was going through the two regions of my lands according to my hearts desire, to see that which I had created, when lo! I was bitten by a serpent which I saw not. Is it fire? Is it water? I am colder than water, I am hotter than fire. All my flesh sweateth, I quake, my eye hath no strength, I cannot see the sky, and the sweat rusheth to my face even as in the time of summer.' Then said Isis unto Râ, 'O tell me thy name, holy Father, for whosoever shall be delivered by thy name shall live.' And Râ said, 'I have made the heavens and the earth, I have knit together the mountains, I have created all that is above them, I have made the water, I have made to come into being the goddess Meht-urt, and I have made the Bull of his mother, from whom spring the delights of love. I have made the heavens, I have stretched out the two horizons like a curtain, and I have placed the soul of the gods within them. I am he who, if he openeth his eyes, doth make the light, and, if he closeth them, darkness cometh into being. At his command the Nile riseth, and the gods know not his name. I have made the hours, I have created the days, I bring forward the festivals of the year, I create the Nile-flood. I make the fire of life, and I provide food in the houses. I am Khepera in the morning, I am Râ at noon, and I am Temu at even.' Meanwhile the poison was not taken away from his body, but it pierced deeper, and the great god could no longer walk.

"Then said Isis unto Râ, 'What thou hast said is not thy name. O tell it unto me, and the poison shall depart; for he shall live whose name shall be revealed! Now the poison burned like fire, and it was fiercer than the flame and the furnace, and the majesty of the great god said, 'I consent that Isis shall search into me, and that my name shall pass from me into her.' Then the god hid himself from the gods, and his place in the Boat of Millions of Years was empty.

And when the time had arrived for the heart of Râ to come forth, Isis spake unto her son Horus, saying, 'The god hath bound himself by oath to deliver up his two eyes (*i.e.*, the sun and moon).' Thus was the name of the great god taken from him, and Isis, the lady of words of magical power, said, 'Depart, poison, go forth from Ea. O Eye of Horus, go forth from the god, and shine outside his mouth. It is I who work, it is I who make to fall down upon the earth the vanquished poison, for the name of the great god hath been taken away from him. Let Râ live, and let the poison die! Let the poison die, and let Râ live!' These are the words of Isis, the mighty lady, the mistress of the gods, who knew Râ by his own name."

Now from a few words of text which follow the above narrative we learn that the object of writing it was not so much to instruct the reader as to make a magic formula, for we are told that it was to be recited over figures of Temu and Horus, and Isis and Horus, that is to say, over figures of Temu the evening sun, Horus the Elder, Horus the son of Isis, and Isis herself. Temu apparently takes the place of Râ, for he represents the sun as an old man, *i.e.*, Râ, at the close of his daily life when he has lost his strength and power. The text is a charm or magical formula against snake bites, and it was thought that the written letters, which represented the words of Isis, would save the life of any one who was snake-bitten, just as they saved the life of Râ. If the full directions as to the use of the figures of Temu, Isis, and the two Horus gods, were known unto us we should probably find that they were to be made to act in dumb show the scenes which took place between Râ, and Isis when the goddess succeeded in taking from him his name. Thus we have ample evidence that Isis possessed marvellous magical powers, and this being so, the issues of life and death, as far as the deceased was concerned, we know from the texts to have been in her hands. Her words of power, too, were a priceless possession, for she obtained them from Thoth, who was the personification of the mind and intelligence of the Creator, and thus their origin was divine, and from this point of view were inspired.

From a papyrus of the Ptolemaic period we obtain some interesting facts about the great skill in working magic and about the knowledge of magical formulae which were possessed by a prince called Setnau Khâ-em-Uast. He knew how to use the powers of amulets and talismans, and how to compose magical formulae, and he was master both of religious literature and of that of the "double house of life," or library of magical books. One day as he was talking of such things one of the king's wise men laughed at his remarks, and in answer Setnau said, "If thou wouldst read a book possessed of magical powers come with me and I will show it to thee, the book was written by Thoth himself, and in it there are two formulae. The recital of the first will enchant (or bewitch) heaven, earth, hell, sea, and mountains, and by it thou shalt see all the birds, reptiles, and fish, for its power will bring the fish to the top of the water. The recital of the second will enable a man if he be in the tomb to take the form which he had upon earth," etc. When questioned as to where the book was, Setnau said that it was in the tomb of Ptah-nefer-ka at Memphis. A little later Setnau went there with his brother and passed three days and three nights in seeking for the tomb of Ptah-nefer-ka, and on the third day they found it; Setnau recited some words over it, and the earth opened and they went down to the place where the book was. When the two brothers came into the tomb they found it to be brilliantly lit up by the light which came forth from the book; and when they looked they saw not only Ptah-nefer-ka, but his wife Ahura, and Merhu their son.

Now Ahura and Merhu were buried at Coptos but their doubles had come to live with Ptah-nefer-ka by means of the magical power of Thoth. Setnau told them that he had come to take away the book, but Ahura begged him not to do so, and related to him the misfortunes which had already followed the possession of it. She was, it seems, the sister of Ptah-nefer-ka whom she married, and after the birth of her son Merhu, her husband seemed to devote himself exclusively to the study of magical books, and one day a priest of Ptah promised to tell him where the magical book described above might be found if he would give him a hundred pieces of silver, and provide him with two handsome coffins. When the money and the coffins had been given to him, the priest of Ptah told Ptah-nefer-ka that the book was in an iron box in the middle of the river at Coptos. "The iron box is in a bronze box, the bronze box is in a box of palm-tree wood, the palm tree wood box is in a box of ebony and ivory, the ebony and ivory box is in a silver box, the silver box is in a gold box, and in the gold (sic) box lies the book. The box wherein is the book is surrounded by swarms of serpents and scorpions and reptiles of all kinds, and round it is coiled a serpent which cannot die." Ptah-nefer-ka told his wife and the king what he had heard, and at length set out for Coptos with Ahura and Merhu in the royal barge; having arrived at Coptos he went to the temple of Isis and Harpocrates and offered up a sacrifice and poured out a libation to these gods. Five days later the high priest of Coptos made for him the model of a floating stage and figures of workmen provided with tools; he then recited words of power over them and they became living, breathing men, and the search for the box began. Having worked for three days and three nights they came to the place where the box was. Ptah-nefer-ka dispersed the serpents and scorpions which were round about the nest of boxes by his words of power, and twice succeeded in killing the serpent coiled round the box, but it came to life again; the third time he cut it into two pieces, and laid sand between them, and this time it did not take its old form again. He then opened the boxes one after the other, and taking out the gold box with the book inside it carried it to the royal barge. He next read one of the two formula, in it and so enchanted or bewitched the heavens and the earth that he learned all their secrets; he read the second and he saw the sun rising in the heavens with his company of the gods, etc. His wife Ahura then read the book and saw all that her husband had seen. Ptah-nefer-ka then copied the writings on a piece of new papyrus, and having covered the papyrus with incense dissolved it in water and drank it; thus he acquired the knowledge which was in the magical book. Meanwhile these acts had stirred the god Thoth to wrath, and he told Râ what Ptah-nefer-ka had done. As a result the decree went forth that Ptah-nefer-ka and his wife and child should never return to Memphis, and on the way back to Coptos Ahura and Merhu fell into the river and were drowned; and while returning to Memphis with the book Ptah-nefer-ka himself was drowned also. Setnau, however, refused to be diverted from his purpose, and he insisted on having the book which he saw in the possession of Ptah-nefer-ka; the latter then proposed to play a game of draughts and to let the winner have the book. The game was for fifty-two points, and although Ptah-nefer-ka tried to cheat Setnau, he lost the game. At this juncture Setnau sent his brother Anhaherurau up to the earth to bring him his talismans of Ptah and his other magical writings, and when he returned he laid them upon Setnau, who straightway flew up to heaven grasping the wonderful book in his hand. As he went up from the tomb light went before him, and the darkness closed in behind him; but Ptah-nefer-ka said to his wife, "I will make him bring back this book soon, with a knife and a rod in his hand and a vessel of fire upon his head." Of the bewitchment of Setnau by a beautiful woman called Tabubu and of his troubles in consequence thereof we need make no mention here: it is sufficient to say that the king ordered him to take the book back to its place, and that the prophecy of Ptah-nefer-ka was fulfilled.

In connexion with the subject of the magical powers of Isis must be briefly mentioned the curious small stelae, with rounded tops, on the front of which are inscribed figures of the god Horus standing upon crocodiles: they are usually known as "cippi of Horus." The largest and finest example of this remarkable class of object is the famous "Metternichstele," which was found in the year 1828 during the building of a cistern in a Franciscan monastery in Alexandria, and was presented by Muhammad Ali Pasha to Prince Metternich. We are fortunately enabled to date the stele, for the name of Nectanebus I., the last but one of the native kings of Egypt, who reigned from B.C. 378 to B.C. 360, occurs on it, and we know from many sources that such a monument could have been produced only about this period. From illustrations of it we see that it is both sculptured and engraved with figures of many of the gods of ancient Egypt, gods well known from the monuments of the earlier dynasties, and also with figures of a series of demons and monsters and animals which have both mythological and magical importance. Many of these are accompanied by texts containing magical formulae, magical names, and mythological allusions. In the principal scene we see Horus, or Harpocrates, standing upon two crocodiles; on his brow is the uraeus, and he wears on the right side of his head the lock of hair emblematic of youth. In his hands he grasps serpents, a lion, and an antelope, and it is clear by the look on his face that he is in no wise afraid of them. Above his head is a bearded head, which is usually said to represent that of Bes. On his right are:- (1) an *utchat*, with human hands and arms; (2) Horus-Râ, hawk-headed, and wearing the sun's disk and uraeus, and standing on a serpent coiled up; (3) Osiris, in the form of a hawk standing upon a sceptre, and wearing the *atef* crown; (4) The goddess Isis standing upon a serpent coiled up; (5) The goddess Nekhebet, in the form of a vulture, standing upon a papyrus sceptre. On his left are:- (1) An *utchat* with human hands and arms; (2) a papyrus standard with plumes and *menats*; (3) the god Thoth standing upon a serpent coiled up; (4) the goddess Uatchet, in the form of a serpent, standing upon a papyrus sceptre. Now Horus typifies youth and strength and the rising sun, and the head above him. is probably intended to represent that of Râ (or Bes) as an old man; the allusion here is clearly to the god who "is old at eventide and who becomes young again." The *utchats* and the figures of the gods symbolize the solar powers and the deities who are masters of the words of power, both in the South and in the North, by which the young god Horus vanquishes all hostile animals, reptiles, and creeping things which live in water and on land. Above and about this scene are several rows of figures of gods and sketches of mythological scenes; many of which are evidently taken from the vignettes of the Book of the Dead, and the object of all of the latter is to prove that light overcomes darkness, that good vanquishes evil, and that renewed life comes after death. The texts which fill all the spaces not occupied by figures describe certain incidents of the eternal combat which Horus wages against his brother

Set, and tell the story of the wanderings of Isis with her son Horus and of her sufferings in the country of the papyrus Swamps; besides these, prayers to certain gods are introduced. The whole monument is nothing but a talisman, or a gigantic amulet engraved with magical figures and words of power, and it was, undoubtedly, placed in some conspicuous place in a courtyard or in a house to protect the building and its inmates from the attacks of hostile beings, visible and invisible, and its power was believed to be invincible. There is not a god of any importance whose figure is not on it, and there is not a demon, or evil animal or reptile, who is not depicted upon it in a vanquished state; the knowledge of the ancient Egyptian mythology and the skill shewn by the designer of this talisman are very remarkable. The small cippi of Horus contain nothing but extracts from the scenes and texts which we find on the "Metternichstele," and it, or similar objects, undoubtedly formed the source from which so many of the figures of the strange gods which are found on Gnostic gems were derived. Certain of the figures of the gods on the cippi were cast in bronze in the Ptolemaic and Roman periods, or hewn in stone, and were buried in tombs and under the foundations of houses to drive away any of the fiends who might come to do harm either to the living or the dead.

The Arab historian Mas'ûdî has preserved a curious legend of the talismans which were employed by Alexander the Great to protect the city of Alexandria whilst it was being built, and as the legend is of Egyptian origin, and dates from a period not greatly removed from that in which the Metternich stele was made, it is worthy of mention. When the foundations of the city had been laid, and the walls had begun to rise up, certain savage animals came up each night from the sea, and threw down everything which had been built during the day; watchmen were appointed to drive them away, but in spite of this each morning saw the work done during the previous day destroyed. After much thought Alexander devised a plan whereby he might thwart the sea monsters, and he proceeded to carry it into effect. He made a box ten cubits long and five cubits wide with sides made of sheets of glass fastened into frames by means of pitch, resin, etc. In this box Alexander placed himself, together with two skilful draughtsmen, and having been closed it was towed out to sea by two vessels; and when weights of iron, lead, and stone had been attached to the under part of it, it began to sink, being guided to the place which Alexander wished it to reach by means of cords which were worked from the ships. When the box touched the bottom of the sea, thanks to the clearness of the glass sides and the water of the sea, Alexander and his two companions were able to watch the various marine monsters which passed by, and he saw that although they had human bodies they had the heads of beasts; some had axes, some had saws, and some had hammers, and they all closely resembled workmen. As they passed in front of the box Alexander and his two draughtsmen copied their forms upon paper with great exactness, and depicted their hideous countenances, and stature, and shape; this done, a signal was made, and the box was drawn up to the surface. As soon as Alexander reached the land he ordered his stone and metal workers to make reproductions of the sea monsters according to the drawings which he and his friends had made, and when they were finished he caused them to be set up on pedestals along the sea-shore, and continued his work of building the city. When the night came, the sea monsters appeared as usual, but as soon as they saw that figures of themselves had been put up on the shore they returned at once to the water and did not shew themselves again. When, however, the city had been built and was inhabited, the sea monsters made their appearance again, and each morning a considerable number of people were found to be missing; to prevent this Alexander placed talismans upon the pillars which, according to Mas'ûdî, were there in his day. Each pillar was in the shape of an arrow and was eighty cubits in height, and rested upon a plinth of brass; the talismans were placed at their bases, and were in the form of figures or statues of certain beings with suitable inscriptions, and as they were put in position after careful astronomical calculations had been made for the purpose we may assume that they produced the effect desired by the king.

CHAPTER V
MAGICAL NAMES

THE Egyptians, like most Oriental nations, attached very great importance to the knowledge of names, and the knowledge of how to use and to make mention of names which possessed magical powers was a necessity both for the living and the dead. It was believed that if a man knew the name of a god or a devil, and addressed him by it, he was bound to answer him and to do whatever he wished; and the possession of the knowledge of the name of a man enabled his neighbour to do him good or evil. The name that was the object of a curse brought down evil upon its owner, and similarly the name that was the object of a blessing or prayer for benefits secured for its master many good things. To the Egyptian the name was as much a part of a man's being as his soul, or his double (*ka*), or his body, and it is quite certain that this view was held by him in the earliest times. Thus in the text which is inscribed on the walls inside the pyramid of Pepi L, king of Egypt about B.C. 3200, we read, "Pepi hath been purified. He hath taken in his hand the *mâh* staff, he hath provided himself with his throne, and he hath taken his seat in the boat of the great and little companies of the gods. Ed maketh Pepi to sail to the West, he stablisheth his seat above those of the lords of doubles, and he writeth down Pepi at the head of those who live. The doors of Pekh-ka which are in the abyss open themselves to Pepi, the doors of the iron which is the ceiling of the sky open themselves to Pepi, and he passeth through them; he hath his panther skin upon him, and the staff and whip are in his hand. Pepi goeth forward with his flesh, Pepi is happy with his name, and he liveth with his *ka* (double)." Curiously enough only the body and name and double of the king are mentioned, just as if these three constituted his whole economy; and it is noteworthy what importance is attached to the name in this passage. In the text from the pyramid of another king we have a prayer concerning the preservation of the name, which is of such interest that a rendering of it in full is here given: it reads, "O Great Company of the gods who dwell in Annu (Heliopolis), grant that Pepi Nefer-ka-Râ may flourish (*literally* 'germinate'), and that his pyramid, his ever lasting building, may flourish, even as the name of Temu, the chief of the nine gods, doth flourish.

If the name of Shu, the lord of the upper shrine in Annu, flourisheth, then Pepi shall flourish, and his pyramid, his everlasting building, shall flourish! If the name of Tefnut, the lady of the lower shrine in Annu, flourisheth, the name of Pepi shall be established, and this his pyramid shall be established to all eternity! If the name of Seb flourisheth at the 'homage of the earth,' then the name of Pepi shall flourish, and this his pyramid shall flourish, and this his building shall flourish unto all eternity! If the name of Nut in the House of Shenth in Annu flourisheth, the name of Pepi shall flourish, and this his pyramid shall flourish, and this his building shall flourish unto all eternity! If the name of Osiris flourisheth in the nome of Abydos, then the name of Pepi shall flourish, and this his pyramid shall flourish, and this his building shall flourish unto all eternity! If the name of Osiris Khent-Amentet flourisheth, then the name of Pepi shall flourish, and this his pyramid shall flourish, and this his building shall flourish unto all eternity! If the name of Set, the dweller in Nubt (Ombos) flourisheth, then the name of Pepi shall flourish, and this his pyramid shall flourish, and this his building shall flourish unto all eternity! If the name of Horus flourisheth, then the name of Pepi shall flourish, and this his pyramid shall flourish, and this his building shall flourish unto all eternity! If the name of Râ flourisheth in the horizon, then the name of

163

Pepi shall flourish, and this his pyramid shall flourish, and this his building shall flourish unto all eternity! If the name of Khent-merti flourisheth in Sekhem (Letopolis), then the name of Pepi shall flourish, and this his pyramid shall flourish, and this his building shall flourish unto all eternity! If the name of Uatchet in Tep flourisheth, then the name of Pepi shall flourish, and this his pyramid shall flourish, and this his building shall flourish unto all eternity!"

The above prayer or formula was the origin of most of the prayers and texts which had for their object the "making the name to germinate or flourish," and which were copied so frequently in the Saïte, Ptolemaic, and Roman periods. All these compositions show that from the earliest to the latest times the belief as to the importance of the preservation of the name never changed in Egypt, and the son who assisted in keeping green his father's name, and in consequence his memory, performed a most meritorious duty. But in the present chapter we are not so much concerned with the ordinary as with the extraordinary uses to which a name might be put, and the above facts have only been mentioned to prove that a man's name was regarded as an essential part of himself, and that the blotting out of the name of an individual was synonymous with his destruction. Without a name no man could be identified in the judgment, and as a man only came into being upon this earth when his name had been pronounced, so the future life could only be attained after the gods of the world beyond the grave had become acquainted with it and had uttered it.

According to the story of the Creation which is related in the Papyrus of Nesi-Amsu, before the world and all that therein is came into being, only the great god Neb-er-tcher existed, for even the gods were not born. Now when the time had come for the god to create all things be says, "I brought (*i.e.*, fashioned) my mouth, and I uttered my own name as a word of power, and thus I evolved myself under the evolutions of the god Khepera, and I developed myself out of the primeval matter which had evolved multitudes of evolutions from the beginning of time. Nothing existed on this earth [before me], I made all things. There was none other who worked with me at that time. Elsewhere, that is to say, in the other version of the story, the god Khepera says, I developed ct myself from the primeval matter which I made, I developed myself out of the primeval matter. My name is Osiris, the germ of primeval matter." Here, then, we have a proof that the Egyptians regarded the creation as the result of the utterance of the name of the god Neb-er-tcher or Khepera by himself. Again, in the story of Râ and Isis, given in the preceding chapter, we have seen that although Isis was able to make a serpent and to cause it to bite Râ, and to make him very ill, she was powerless to do as she wished in heaven and upon earth until she had persuaded the god to reveal to her his name by which he ruled the universe. In yielding up his name to the goddess he placed himself in her power, and in this example we have a striking instance of the belief that the knowledge of the name of god, or devil, or human being, implied dominion over that being. We have seen elsewhere that Râ, the type and symbol of God, is described as the god of "many names," and in that wonderful composition the XVIIth Chapter of the Book of the Dead, we have the following statement:- "I am the great god Nu, who gave birth unto himself, and who made his name to become the company of the gods." Then the question, "What does this mean?" or "Who is this?" is asked. And this is the answer: "It is Râ, the creator of the name[s] of his limbs, which came into being in the form of the gods who are in the following of Râ." From this we see that all the "gods" of Egypt were merely personifications of the names of Râ, and that each god was one of his members, and that a name of a god was the god himself. Without the knowledge of the names of the gods and devils of the underworld the dead Egyptian would have fared badly, for his personal liberty would have been fettered, the roads and paths would have been blocked to him, the gates of the mansions of the underworld would have been irrevocably shut in his face, and the hostile powers which dogged his footsteps would have made an end of him; these facts are best illustrated by the following examples:-

When the deceased comes to the Hall of Judgment, at the very beginning of his speech he says, "Homage to thee, O Great God, thou Lord of Maâti, I have come to thee, O my Lord, and I have brought myself hither that 1 may behold thy beauties. I know thee, and I know thy name, and I know the names of the two and forty gods who exist with thee in this Hall of Maâti."But although the gods may be favourable to him, and he be found righteous in the judgment, he cannot make his way among the other gods of the underworld without a knowledge of the names of certain parts of the Hall of Maâti. After the judgment he acquires the mystical name of "He who is equipped with the flowers and the dweller in his olive tree," and it is only after he has uttered this name that the gods say "Pass onwards." Next the gods invite him to enter the Hall of Maâti, but he is not allowed to pass in until he has, in answer to questions asked by the bolts, lintels, threshold, fastenings, socket, door-leaves, and door-posts, told their names. The floor of the Hall will not permit him to walk upon it unless he tells not only its name, but also the mystical names of his two legs and feet wherewith he is about to tread upon it. When all this has been done the guardian of the Hall says to him, "I will not announce thy name [to the god] unless thou tellest me my name"; and the deceased replies, "'Discerner of hearts and searcher of the reins' is thy name." In reply to this the guardian says, "If I announce thy name thou must utter the name of the god who dwelleth in his hour," and the deceased utters the name "Mâau-Taui." But still the guardian is not satisfied, and he says, "If I announce thy name thou must tell me who is he whose heaven is of fire, whose walls [are surmounted by] living uraei, and the floor of whose house is a stream of water. Who is he, I say? (i.e., what is his name?)" But the deceased has, of course, learnt the name of the Great God, and he replies, "Osiris." The guardian of the Hall is now content, and he says, "Advance, verily thy name shall be mentioned to him"; and he further promises that the cakes, and ale, and sepulchral meals which the deceased shall enjoy shall come from the "Eye of Râ,"

In another Chapter the deceased addresses seven gods, and says, "Hail, ye seven beings who make decrees, who support the Balance on the night of the judgment of the Utchat, who cut off heads, who hack necks in pieces, who take possession of hearts by violence and rend the places where hearts are fixed, who make slaughterings in the Lake of Fire, I know you, and I know your names; therefore know ye me, even as I know your names." The deceased, having declared that the seven gods know his name and he their names, has no further apprehension that evil will befall him.

In one portion of the kingdom of Osiris there existed seven halls or mansions through which the deceased was anxious to pass, but each of the gates was guarded by a doorkeeper, a watcher, and a herald, and it required special provision on the part of the deceased to satisfy these beings that he had a right to pass them. In the first place, figures of the seven gates had to be made in some substance (or painted upon papyrus), as well as a figure of the deceased: the latter was made to approach each of the gates and to stand before it and to recite an address which had been specially prepared for the purpose. Meanwhile the thigh, the head, the heart, and the hoof of a red bull were offered at each gate, as well as a very large number of miscellaneous offerings which need not be described in detail. But all these ceremonies would not help the deceased to pass through the gates, unless he knew the names of the seven doorkeepers, and the seven watchers, and the seven heralds who guarded them. The gods of the first gate were:- Sekhet-hra-âsht-aru, Semetu, and Hukheru; those of the second, Tun-hât, Seqet-hra, and Sabes; of the third, Am-huat-ent-pehfi, Res-hra, and Uâau; of the fourth, Khesef-hra-âsht-kheru, Res-ab, and Neteka-hra-khesef-atu; of the fifth, Ânkh-em-fentu, Ashebu, and Tebherkehaat; of the sixth, Akentauk-ha-kheru, An-hra, and Metes-hra-ari-she; of the seventh, Metes-sen, Ââa-kheru, and Khesef-hra-khemiu. And the text, which the deceased recites to the Halls collectively, begins, "Hail, ye Halls! Hail, ye who made the Halls for Osiris! Hail, ye who watch your Halls! Hail, ye who herald the affairs of the two lands for the god Osiris each day, the deceased knoweth you, and he knoweth your names." The names having been uttered, and the addresses duly recited, the deceased went wherever he pleased in the seven Halls of Osiris.

But beside the seven halls the deceased had to pass through the twenty-one hidden pylons of the house of Osiris in the Elysian Fields, and in order to do so he had to declare the names of the pylon and the doorkeeper of each, and to make a short address besides. Thus to the first pylon he says, "I have made my way, I know thee and I know thy name, and I know the name of the god who guardeth thee. Thy name is 'Lady of tremblings, with lofty walls, the sovereign lady, the mistress of destruction, who setteth in order the words which drive back the whirlwind and the storm, who delivereth from destruction him that travelleth along the way'; and the name of thy doorkeeper is Neri." At the second pylon he says, "I have made [my] way, I know thee, and I know thy name, and I know the name of the god who guardeth thee. Thy name is 'Lady of heaven, the mistress of the world, who devoureth with fire, the lady of mortals, who knoweth mankind.' The name of thy doorkeeper is Mes-Ptah," and so on at each of the pylons. In the later and longer version of the chapter which was written to supply the deceased with this knowledge he informs the god of each pylon what purification he has undergone; thus to the god of the first pylon he says, "I have anointed myself with *hâti* "unguent [made from] the cedar, I have arrayed myself in apparel of *menkh* (linen), and I have with me my sceptre made of *heti* wood." After the speech the god of the pylon says, "Pass on, then, thou art pure."

When we remember that one of the oldest beliefs as to the future life made it appear that it would be lived by man in the Sekhet-Aaru, or Field of Reeds, a region which, as we know from the drawings of it which have come down to us, was intersected by canals and streams, it is at once clear that in order to pass from one part of it to another the deceased would need a boat. Even assuming that he was fortunate enough to have made his own way into this region, it was not possible for him to take a boat with him. To meet this difficulty a boat and all its various parts were drawn upon the papyrus, upon which the selection of Chapters from the Book of the Dead had been inscribed for him, and a knowledge of the text of the chapter which belonged to it made the drawing to become an actual boat. But before he could enter it, the post to which it was tied up, and every part of the boat itself, demanded that he should tell them their names, thus:-

Post at which to tie up. "Tell me my name." D. "Lord of the two lands, dweller in the shrine," is thy name.

Rudder. "Tell me my name." D. "Leg of Hâpiu" is thy name.

Rope. "Tell me my name." D. "Hairs with which Anpu finisheth the work of my embalmment" is thy name.

Oar-ruts. "Tell us our name." D. "Pillars of the underworld" is your name.

Hold. "Tell me my name." D. "Akau" is thy name.

Mast. "Tell me my name." D. "Bringer back of the lady after her departure" is thy name.

Lower deck. "Tell me my name." D. "Standard of Ap-uat" is thy name.

Upper Post. "Tell me my name." D. "Throat of Mestha" is thy name.

Sail. "Tell me my name." D. "Nut" is thy name.

Leather Straps. "Tell us our name." D. "Those who are made from the hide of the Mnevis Bull, which was burned by Suti," is your name.

Paddles. "Tell us our name." D. "Fingers of Horus the firstborn" is your name.

Pump (?). "Tell me my name." D. "The hand of Isis which wipeth away the blood of the Eye of Horus," is thy name.

Planks. "Tell us our names." D. "Mestha, Hâpi, Tuamutef, Qebhsennuf, Haqau, Thet-em-âua, Maa-an-tef, Ari-nef-tchesef," are your names.

Rows. "Tell us our name." D. "He who is at the head of his nomes" is your name.

Hull. "Tell me my name." D. "Mert" is thy name.

Rudder. "Tell me my name." D. "Âqa" is thy name; Shiner in the water, hidden beam," is thy name.

Keel. "Tell me my name." D. "Thigh of Isis, which Râ cut off with the knife to bring blood into the Sektet boat," is thy name.

Sailor. "Tell me my name." D. "Traveller" is thy name.

Wind. "Tell me my name." D. "The North Wind, which cometh from Tem to the nostrils of Osiris," is thy name.

And when the deceased had declared to these their names, before he could set out on his journey he was obliged to tell the river, and the river-banks, and the ground their mystical names. This done, the boat admitted him as a passenger, and he was able to sail about to any part of the Elysian Fields at will.

But among the beings whom the deceased wished to avoid in the underworld were the beings who "lay snares, and who work the nets, and who are fishers," and who would draw him into their nets. It seems as if it were absolutely necessary that he should fall in with these beings and their nets, for a whole chapter of the Book of the Dead was written with the view of enabling him to escape from them unharmed; the god their leader is called "the god whose face is behind him," and "the god who hath gained the mastery over his heart." To escape from the net which was worked by "the fishers who lay snares with their nets and who go round about in the chambers of the waters," the deceased had to know the names of the net, and of the ropes, and of the pole, and of the hooks, and of each and every part of it; without this knowledge nothing could save him from calamity. We unfortunately understand very few of the allusions to mythological events which are contained in the names of the various parts of the machinery which work the net, but it is quite certain that they have reference to certain events in the lives of the gods who are mentioned, and that these were well known to the writers and readers of religious texts.

From the above descriptions of the means whereby the deceased made his way through the gates and the halls of the underworld and escaped from the fowler and his net, it will be readily understood that the knowledge of the name alone was, in some cases, sufficient to help him out of his difficulties; but in others it was necessary to have the name which was possessed of magical power inscribed upon some object, amulet or otherwise. Moreover, some gods and devils were thought to have the power to assume different forms, and as each form carried with it its own name, to have absolute power over a god of many forms it was necessary to know all his names. Thus in the "Book of Overthrowing Âpep" we are told not only to make a wax figure of the monster, but also to write his name upon it, so that when the figure is destroyed by being burnt in the fire his name also may be destroyed; this is a striking example of the belief that the name was an integral part of the economy of a living creature. But Âpep possessed many forms and therefore many names, and unless he could be invoked by these names he still had the power to do evil; the above-mentioned book therefore supplies us with a list of his names, among which occur the following:- "Tutu (*i.e.*, Doubly evil one), Hau-hra (*i.e.*, Backward Face), Hemhemti (*i.e.*, Roarer), Qetu (*i.e.*, Evil-doer), Âmam (*i.e.*, Devourer), Saatet-ta (*i.e.*, Darkener of earth), Iubani, Khermuti, Unti, Karauememti, Khesef-hra, Sekhem-hra,

Khak-ab, Nâi, Uai, Beteshu, Kharebutu the fourfold fiend,"
etc. All these names represent, as may be seen from the few
of which translations are given, various aspects of Âpep,
the devil of thunder, lightning, cloud, rain, mist, storm,
and the like, and the anxiety to personify these so that the
personifications might be attacked by means of magical
ceremonies and words of power seems positively childish.

Passing now to certain chapters of the Book of the
Dead which are rich in names of magical power, we notice
that the god Amen, whose name meant the "hidden one,"
possessed numerous names, upon the knowledge of which
the deceased relied for protection. Thus he says, "O Amen,
Amen; O Re-Iukasa; O God, Prince of the gods of the east,
thy name is Na-ari-k, or (as others say) Ka-ari-ka, Kasaika
is thy name. Arethikasathika is thy name. Amen-na-an-ka-
entek-share, or (as others say) Thek-share-Amen-kerethi, is
thy name. O Amen, let me make supplication unto thee, for I,
even I, know thy name. Amen is thy name. Ireqai is thy name.
Marqathai is thy name. Rerei is thy name. Nasaqbubu is thy
name. Thanasa-Thanasa is thy name. Shareshatha-katha is
thy name. O Amen, O Amen, O God, O God, O Amen, I
adore thy name." In another place the deceased addresses
Sekhet-Bast-Râ, saying, "Thou art the fire-goddess Ami-
seshet, whose opportunity escapeth her not; thy name is
Kaharesapusaremkakaremet, Thou art like unto the mighty

flame of Saqenaqat which is in the bow of the boat of thy father Harepukakashareshabaiu, for behold, thus is [the name uttered] in the speech of the Negroes, and of the Anti, and of the people of Nubia. Sefiperemhesihrahaputchetef is thy name; Atareamtcherqemturennuparsheta is the name of one of thy divine sons, and Panemma that of the other." And in yet another chapter the deceased addressing the god Par says, "Thou art the mighty one of names among the gods, the mighty runner whose strides are might thou art the god the mighty one who comest and rescuest the needy one and the afflicted from him that oppresseth him; give heed to my cry. I am the Cow, and thy divine name is in my mouth, and I will utter it; Haqabakaher is thy name; Âurauaaqersaanqrebathi is thy name; Kherserau is thy name; Kharsatha is thy name. I praise thy name ... . O be gracious unto the deceased, and cause thou heat to exist under his head, for, indeed, he is the soul of the great divine Body which resteth in Annu (Heliopolis), whose names are Khukheperuru and Barekathatchara."

The examples of the use of names possessing magical powers described above illustrate the semi-religious views on the subject of names which the Egyptians held, and we have now to consider briefly the manner in which the knowledge of a name was employed in uses less important than those which had for their object the attainment of life and happiness in the world to come. In the famous magical papyrus which Chabas published we find a series of interesting charms and magical formulae which were written to preserve its possessor from the attacks of sea and river monsters of every kind, of which the following is an example. "Hail, lord of the gods! Drive away from me the lions of the country of Meru (Meroë?), and the crocodiles which come forth from the river, and the bite of all poisonous reptiles which crawl forth from their holes. Get thee back, O crocodile Mâk, thou son of Set! Move not by means of thy tail! Work not thy legs and feet! Open not thy mouth! Let the water which is before thee turn into a consuming fire, O thou whom the thirty-seven gods did make, and whom the serpent of Râ did put in chains, O thou who wast fettered with links of iron before the boat of Râ! Get thee back, O crocodile Mâk, thou son of Set!" These words were to be said over a figure of the god Amen painted on clay; the rod was to have four rams' heads upon one neck, under his feet was to be a figure of the crocodile Mâk, and to the right and left of him were to be the dog headed apes, *i.e.*, the transformed spirits of the dawn, who sang hymns of praise to Râ when he rose daily. Again, let us suppose that some water monster wished to attack a man in a boat. To avoid this the man stood before the cabin of the boat and, taking a hard egg in his hand, he said, "O egg of the water which hath been spread over the earth, essence of the divine apes, the great one in the heaven above and in the earth beneath, who dost dwell in the nests which are in the waters, I have come forth with thee from the water, I have been with thee in thy nest, I am Amsu of Coptos, I am Amsu, lord of Kebu." When he had said these words he would appear to the animal in the water in the form of the god Amsu, with whom he had identified himself, and it would be afraid and flee. At the end of the papyrus in which the above extracts occur we find a series of magical names which may be read thus:- Atir-Atisa, Atirkaha-Atisa, Samumatnatmu-Atisa, Samuanemui-Atisa, Samutekaari-Atisa, Samutekabaiu-Atisa, Samutchakaretcha-Atisa, Tâuuarehasa, Qina, Hama, Senentuta-Batetsataiu, Anrehakatha-sataiu, Haubailra-Haari. From these and similar magical names it is quite certain that the Gnostics and other sects which held views akin to theirs obtained the names which they were so fond of inscribing upon their amulets and upon the so-called magical papyri. The last class of documents undoubtedly contains a very large proportion of the magical ideas, beliefs, formulae, etc., which were current in Egypt from the time of the Ptolemies to the end of the Roman Period, but from about B.C. 150 to A.D. 200 the papyri exhibit traces of the influence of Greek, Hebrew, and Syrian philosophers and magicians, and from a passage like the following we may get a proof of this:- "I call thee, the headless one, that didst create earth and heaven, that didst create night and day, thee the creator of light and darkness. Thou art Osoronnophris, whom no man hath seen at any time; thou art Iabas, thou art Iapôs, thou hast distinguished the just and the unjust, thou didst make female and male, thou didst produce seeds and fruits, thou didst make men to love one another and to bate one another. I am Moses thy prophet, to whom thou didst commit thy mysteries, the ceremonies of Israel; thou didst produce the moist and the dry and all manner of food. Listen to me: I am an angel of Phapro Osoronnophris; this is thy true name, handed down to the prophets of Israel. Listen to me…" In this passage the name Osoronnophris is clearly a corruption of the old Egyptian names of the great god of the dead "Ausar Unnefer," and Phapro seems to represent the Egyptian *Per-âa* (literally, "great house") or "Pharaoh," with the article *pa* "the" prefixed. It is interesting to note that Moses is mentioned, a fact which seems to indicate Jewish influence.

In another magical formula we read, "I call upon thee that didst create the earth and bones, and all flesh and all spirit, that didst establish the sea and that shakest the heavens, that didst divide the light from the darkness, the great regulative mind, that disposest everything, eye of the world, spirit of spirits, god of gods, the lord of spirits, the immoveable Aeon, IAOOUÊI, hear my voice. I call upon thee, the ruler of the gods, high-thundering Zeus, Zeus, king, Adonai, lord, Iaoouêe. I am he that invokes thee in the Syrian tongue, the great god, Zaalaêr, Iphphou, do thou not disregard the Hebrew appellation Ablanathanalb, Abrasilôa. For I am Silthakhôoukh, Lailam, Blasalôth, Iaô, Ieô, Nebouth, Sabiothar, Bôth, Arbathiaô, Iaoth, Sabaôth, Patoure, Zagourê, Baroukh Adonai, Elôai, Iabraam, Barbarauô, Nau, Siph," etc. The spell ends with the statement that it "loosens chains, blinds, brings dreams, creates favour; it may be used in common for whatever purpose you will." In the above we notice at once the use of the seven vowels which form "a name wherein be contained all Names, and all Lights, and all Powers." The seven vowels have, of course, reference to the three vowels "Iaô" which were intended to represent one of the Hebrew names for Almighty God, "Jâh." The names "Adonai, Elôai," are also derived through the Hebrew from the Bible, and Sabaôth is another well-known Hebrew word meaning "hosts"; some of the remaining names could be explained, if space permitted, by Hebrew and Syriac words. On papyri and amulets the vowels are written in magical combinations in such a manner as to form triangles and other shapes; with them are often found the names of the seven archangels of God; the following are examples:-

In combination with a number of signs which owe their origin to the Gnostics the seven vowels were sometimes engraved upon plaques, or written upon papyri, with the view of giving the possessor power over gods or demons or his fellow creatures. The example printed below is found on a papyrus in the British Museum and accompanies a spell written for the-purpose of overcoming the malice of enemies, and for giving security against alarms and nocturnal visions.

Amulet inscribed with signs and letters of magical power for overcoming the malice of enemies. (From Brit. Mus., Greek Papyrus, Nu. CXXIV. 4th or 5th century.)

But of all the names found upon Gnostic gems two,

i.e., Khnoubis (or Khnumis/Khnoumis), and Abrasax (or Abraxas), are of the most frequent occurrence. The first is usually represented as a huge serpent having the head of

αξηιουω	μιχαηλ
εηιουωα	ραφαηλ
ηιουωαξ	γαβριηλ
ιουωαξη	σουριηλ
ουωαξηι	ζαζιηλ
υωαξηιο	βαδακιηλ
ωαξηιου	συλιηλ

a lion surrounded by seven or twelve rays. Over the seven rays, one on the point of each, are the seven vowels of the Greek alphabet, which some suppose to refer to the seven heavens; and on the back of the amulet, on which the figure of Khnoumis occurs, is usually found the sign of the triple S and bar. Khnoumis is, of course, a form of the ancient Egyptian god Khnemu, or "Fashioner" of man and beast, the god to whom many of the attributes of the Creator of the universe were ascribed. Khnemu is, however, often depicted with the head of a ram, and in the later times, as the "beautiful ram of Râ," he has four heads; in the Egyptian monuments he has at times the head of a hawk, but never that of a lion. The god Abrasax is represented in a form which has a human body, the bead of a hawk or cock, and legs terminating in serpents; in one hand he holds a knife or dagger, and in the other a shield upon which is inscribed the great name IAΩ {Greek *IAW*}, or JÂH. Considerable difference of opinion exists as to the meaning and derivation of the name Abrasax, but there is no doubt that the god who bore it was a form of the Sun-god, and that he was intended to represent some aspect of the Creator of the world. The name was believed to possess magical powers of the highest class, and Basileides, who gave it currency in the second century, seems to have regarded it as an invincible name. It is probable, however, that its exact meaning was lost at an early date, and that it soon degenerated into a mere magical symbol, for it is often found inscribed on amulets side by side with scenes and figures with which, seemingly, it cannot have any connexion whatever. Judging from certain Gnostic gems in the British Museum, Abrasax is to be identified with the polytheistic figure that stands in the upper part of the Metternich stele. This figure has two bodies, one being that of a man, and the other that of a bird; from these extend four wings, and from each of his knees projects a serpent. He has two pairs of hands and arms; one pair is extended along the wings, each hand holding the symbols of "life," "stability," and "power," and two knives and two serpents; the other pair is pendent, the right hand grasping the sign of life, and the other a sceptre. His face is grotesque, and probably represents that of Bes, or the sun as an old man; on his head is a pylon-shaped object with figures of various animals, and above it a pair of horns which support eight knives and the figure of a god with raised hands and arms, which typifies "millions of years." The god stands upon an oval wherein are depicted figures of various "typhonic" animals, and from each side of his crown proceed several symbols of fire. Whether in the Gnostic system Abraxas absorbed all the names and attributes of this god of many forms cannot be said with certainty.

CHAPTER VI
MAGICAL CEREMONIES

IN the preceding pages we have seen how the Egyptians employed magical stones or amulets, and magical words, and magical pictures, and magical names, in the performance of deeds both good and evil; it remains to consider these magical ceremonies in which the skill of the magician-priest was exerted to its fullest extent, and with the highest objects, that is to say, to preserve the human body in a mummified condition, and to perform the symbolic acts which would restore its natural functions. When we think of the sublime character of the life which the souls of the blessed dead were believed to lead in heaven with the gods, it is hard to understand why the Egyptians took such pains to preserve the physical body from decay. No Egyptian who believed his Scriptures ever expected that his corruptible body would ascend into heaven and live with the gods, for they declare in no uncertain manner that it remains upon the earth whilst the soul dwells in heaven. But that the preservation of the body was in some way or for some reason absolutely necessary is certain, for the art of mummification flourished for several thousands of years, and unless there was some good reason, besides the observance of conservative custom and traditional use, why it should do so, king and priest, gentle and simple, and rich and poor, would never have burdened their relatives and heirs with the expense of costly funeral ceremonies, and with the performance of rites which were of no avail. At first sight, too, it seems strange to find the Egyptians studying carefully how best to provide the dead with a regular supply of sepulchral offerings, for when we come to think about it we notice that in arranging for the well-being of the dead nothing whatever was left to chance. For example, a papyrus will contain several prayers and pictures with appropriate formulae, the object of each of which is to give the deceased meat and drink; any one of these would have been enough for the purpose, but it was thought best in such an important matter to make assurance doubly sure, and if there was the least doubt about the efficacy of one Chapter one or more of the same class were added. Similarly, the tendency of the natural body after death being to decay, the greatest care was taken in mummifying its various members, lest perchance any one of them should be neglected accidentally, and should, either by the omission of the words of power that ought to have been said over it, or through the lax performance of some ceremony, decay and perish. The Egyptian declared that he was immortal, and believed that he would enjoy eternal life in a spiritual body; yet he attempted by the performance of magical ceremonies and the recital of words of power to make his corruptible body to endure for ever. He believed that he would feed upon the celestial and imperishable food whereon the gods lived, but at the same time he spared no effort or expense to provide for his tomb being supplied at stated intervals throughout the year with perishable food in the shape of offerings of oxen, feathered fowl, cakes, bread, and the like. He mummified his dead and swathed them in linen bandages, and then by the performance of magical ceremonies and by the recital of words of power sought to give back to their members the strength to eat, and drink, and talk, and think, and move at will. Indeed, all the evidence now forthcoming seems to prove that he never succeeded in bringing himself to think that the gods could do without his help, or that the pictures or representations of the scenes which took place in the life, and death, and burial, and resurrection of Osiris, upon which he relied so implicitly, could possibly fail to be as efficacious as the actual power of the god himself.

The examination of mummies has shown us with tolerable clearness what methods were adopted in preparing bodies for bandaging and final ornamentation, and the means adopted for disposing of the more corruptible portions of the body are well known from classical and other writers. But for an account of the manner in which the body was bandaged, and a list of the unguents and other materials employed in the process, and the words of power which were spoken as each bandage was laid in its place, we must have recourse to a very interesting papyrus which has been edited and translated by M. Maspero under the title of *Le Rituel de l'Embaumement*. The first part of the papyrus, which probably gave instructions for the evisceration of the body, is wanting, and only the section which refers to the bandaging is at all perfect. The text opens with an address to the deceased in which it is said, "The perfume of Arabia hath been brought to thee to make perfect thy smell through the scent of the god. Here are brought to thee liquids which have come forth from Râ, to make perfect ... thy smell in the Hall [of Judgment]. O sweet-smelling soul of the great god, thou dost contain such a sweet odour that thy face shall neither change nor perish... Thy members shall become young in Arabia, and thy soul shall appear over thy body in Ta-neter (*i.e.*, the 'divine land')." After this the priest or mummifier was to take a vase of liquid which contained ten perfumes, and to smear therewith the body from head to foot twice, taking especial care to anoint the head thoroughly. He was then to say, "Osiris (*i.e.*, the deceased), thou hast received the perfume which shall make thy members perfect. Thou receivest the source [of life] and thou takest the form of the great Disk (*i.e.*, Aten), which uniteth itself unto thee to give enduring form to thy members; thou shalt unite with Osiris in the great Hall. The unguent cometh unto thee to fashion thy members and to gladden thy heart, and thou shalt appear in the form of Râ; it shall make thee to be sound when thou settest in the sky at eventide, and it shall spread abroad the smell of thee in the nomes of Aqert... . Thou receivest the oil of the cedar in Amentet, and the cedar which came forth from Osiris cometh unto thee; it delivereth thee from thy enemies, and it protecteth thee in the nomes. Thy soul alighteth upon the venerable sycamores. Thou criest to Isis, and Osiris heareth thy voice, and Anubis cometh unto thee to invoke thee. Thou receivest the oil of the country of Manu which hath come from the East, and Râ riseth upon thee at the gates of the horizon, at the holy doors of Neith. Thou goest therein, thy soul is in the upper heaven, and thy body is in the lower heaven ... O Osiris, may the Eye of Horus cause that which floweth forth from it to come to thee, and to thy heart for ever!"

These words having been said, the whole ceremony was repeated, and then the internal organs which had been removed from the body were placed in the "liquid of the children of Horus," so that the liquid of this god might enter into them, and whilst they were being thus treated a chapter was read over them and they were put in the funeral chest. When this was done the internal organs were placed on the body, and the body having been made to lie straight the backbone was immersed in holy oil, and the face of the deceased was turned towards the sky; the bandage of Sebek and Sedi was then laid upon the backbone. In a long speech the deceased is addressed and told that the liquid is "secret," and that it is an emanation of the gods Shu and Seb, and that the resin of Phoenicia and the bitumen of Byblos will make his burial perfect in the underworld, and give him his legs, and facilitate his movements, and sanctify his steps in the Hall of Seb. Next gold, silver, lapis-lazuli, and turquoise are brought to the deceased, and crystal to lighten his face, and carnelian to strengthen his steps; these form amulets which will secure for him a free passage in the underworld. Meanwhile the backbone is kept in oil, and the face of the deceased is turned towards the heavens; and next the gilding of the nails of the fingers and toes begins. When this has been done, and portions of the fingers have been wrapped in linen made at Saïs, the following address is made to the deceased:- "O Osiris, thou receivest thy nails of gold, thy fingers of gold, and thy thumb of *smu* (or *uasm*) metal; the liquid of Râ entereth into thee as well as into the divine members of Osiris, and thou journeyest on thy legs to the immortal abode. Thou hast carried thy hands to the house of eternity, thou art made perfect in gold, thou dost shine brightly in *smu* metal, and thy fingers shine in the dwelling of Osiris, in the sanctuary of Horus himself. O Osiris, the gold of the mountains cometh to thee; it is a holy talisman of the gods in their abodes, and it lighteneth thy face in the lower heaven. Thou breathest in gold, thou appearest in *smu* metal, and the dwellers in Re-stau receive thee; those who are in the funeral chest rejoice because thou hast transformed thyself into a hawk of gold by means of thy amulets (or talismans) of the City of Gold," etc. When these words have been said, a priest who is made to personify Anubis comes to the deceased and performs certain symbolical ceremonies by his head, and lays certain bandages upon it. When the head and mouth and face have been well oiled the bandage of Nekheb is laid on the forehead, the bandage of Hathor on the face, the bandage of Thoth upon the two ears, and the bandage of Nebt-hetep on the nape of the neck. Over the head was laid the bandage of Sekhet, in two pieces, and over each ear, and each nostril, and each cheek was fastened a bandage or strip of linen; over the forehead went four pieces of linen, on the top of the head two, outside the mouth two, and inside two, over the chin two, and over the nape of the neck four large pieces; there were to be twenty-two pieces to the right and to the left of the face passing over the two ears. The Lady of the West is then addressed in these words:- "Grant thou that breathing may take place in the head of the deceased in the underworld, and that he may see with his eyes, and that he may hear with his two ears; and that he may breathe through his nose; and that he may be able to utter sounds with his mouth; and that he may be able to speak with his tongue in the underworld. Receive thou his voice in the Hall of Maâti and his speech in the Hall of Seb in the presence of the Great God, the lord of Amentet." The addresses which follow these words have, reference to the delights and pleasures of the future life which shall be secured for him through the oil and unguents, which are duly specified and described, and through the magical figures which are drawn upon the bandages. The protecting properties of the turquoise and other precious stones are alluded to, and after a further anointing with oil and the placing of grains of myrrh and resin, the deceased is declared to have "received his head," and he is promised that it shall nevermore depart from him. On the conclusion of the ceremonies which concern the head, the deceased has the power to go in among the holy and perfect spirits, his name is exalted among men, the denizens of heaven receive his soul, the beings of the underworld bow down before his body, the dwellers upon earth adore him, and the inhabitants of the funeral mountain renew for him his youth. Besides these things, Anubis and Horus make perfect his bandages, and the god Thoth protects his members by his words of magical power; and he himself has learned the magical formulae which are necessary to make his path straight in the underworld, and also the proper way in which to utter them. All these benefits were secured for him by the use of bandages and unguents which possess both magical names and properties, and by the words of power uttered by the priests who recited the Ritual of Embalmment, and by the ceremonies which the priest who personated Anubis performed beside the body of the deceased in imitation of those which the god Anubis performed for the dead god Osiris in remote days.

Next the left hand of the deceased was mummified and bandaged according to the instructions given in the Ritual of Embalmment. The hand was stretched out on a piece of linen, and a ring was passed over the fingers; it was then filled with thirty-six of the substances which were used in embalming, according to the number of the forms of the god Osiris. This done, the hand was bandaged with a strip of linen in six folds, upon which were drawn figures of Isis and Hâpi. The right hand was treated in a similar way, only the figures drawn upon the bandages were those of Râ and Amsu; and when the appropriate words had been recited over both hands divine protection was assured them. After these things the ceremonies concerning the right and left arms were performed, and these were followed by rubbing the soles of the feet and the legs and the thighs, first with black-stone oil, and secondly with holy oil. The toes were wrapped in linen, and a piece of linen was laid on each leg; on each piece was drawn the figure of a jackal, that on the right leg representing Anubis, and that on the left Horus. When flowers of the ânkham plant and other substances had been laid beside and on the legs, and they had been treated with ebony-gum water and holy oil, and appropriate addresses had been said, the ceremony of bandaging the body was ended. Everything that could be done to preserve the body was now done, and every member of it was, by means of the words of power which changed perishable substances into imperishable, protected to all eternity; when the final covering of purple or white linen had been fastened upon it, the body was ready for the tomb.

But the Ritual of Embalmment which has been briefly described above seems to belong to a late period of Egyptian history, and although the ideas and beliefs contained in it are as old as Egyptian civilization itself, it seems as if it was intended to take the place of a much older and more elaborate work which was in use as far back as the period in which the Great Pyramid was built, and which was intended to be recited during the performance of a complex series of ceremonies, some of which are still not completely understood. It seems as if the performance of all the ceremonies would require several days, and it is clear that only the wealthy could afford the expense which must have attended such elaborate obsequies; for the poorer classes of men the various ceremonies must have been greatly curtailed, and at a very early period we find that a shortened form of ritual had taken their place. Of all the ceremonies, the most important was that of the "Opening of the Mouth and Eyes," which was performed either on the mummy itself or upon a statue which represented it. It has already been stated that the Egyptians believed that they could transmit to a statue the attributes of the person in whose image it was made, and similarly that that which was done to the statue of the mummified person was also done to it. The use of a statue instead of the actual mummy has obvious advantages, for the ceremony could be performed at any time and in any place, and the presence of the mummy was unnecessary. As a matter of fact the ceremony was performed in a chamber at the entrance to the tomb, or outside the tomb at a place which had been made ceremonially pure or consecrated, and those who took part in it were:- (1) The *Kher-heb*, or chief officiating priest, who held a roll of papyrus in his hand. (2) The *Sem* priest. (3) The *Smer*, who was, perhaps, some intimate friend of the deceased. (4) *The Sa-mer-ef*, or man who was either the son of the deceased or his representative. (5) The *Tcherau-ur*, or woman who represented Isis. (6) The *Tcherau-sheraut*, or woman who represented Nephthys. (7) The *Menhu*, or slaughterer. (8) The *Am-asi* priest. (9) The *Am-khent* priest. (10) A number of people who represented the armed guard of Horus. All these became actors in scenes which were intended to represent the events which took place in connexion with the burial of Osiris, with whom the deceased is now identified; the two women took the parts of the goddesses Isis and Nephthys, and the men those of the gods who helped them in the performance of their pious duties. From the scenes which accompany the texts relating to the ceremony of opening the mouth and eyes we see that it began with the sprinkling of water round about the statue or mummy from four vessels, one for each quarter of the earth, and with the recital of addresses to the gods Horus, Set, Thoth, and Sept; this act restored to the deceased the use of his head. The sprinkling of water was followed by a purification by means of incense, also contained in four vases, one for each of the four quarters of the earth. The burning of this sweet-smelling substance assisted in opening the mouth of the deceased and in strengthening his heart. At this stage the *Sem* priest dressed himself in the skin of a cow, and lying down upon a kind of couch pretended to be asleep; but he was roused up by the *Am-asi* priest in the presence of the *Kher-heb* and the *Am-khent* priest, and when the *Sem* priest had seated himself upon a seat, the four men together represented the four children of Horus, or the gods with the heads of a hawk, an ape, a jackal, and a man respectively. The *Sem* priest then said, "I have seen my father in all his forms," which the other men in turn repeat. The meaning of this portion of the ceremony is hard to explain, but M. Maspero thinks that it was intended to bring back to the body of the deceased its shadow (*khaibit*), which had departed from it when it died. The preliminary purifications being ended, and the shadow having been joined to the body once more, the statue or mummy is approached by the men who represent the armed guard of Horus; and one of their number, having taken upon himself the character of Horus, the son of Osiris and Isis, touches its mouth with his finger. The *Kher-heb* next made ready to perform the sacrifice which was intended to commemorate the slaughter, at some very early period, of the fiends who were the friends of Set. It seems that, the soul of Horus dwelt in an eye, and that Set nearly succeeded in devouring it; but Horus vanquished Set and saved his eye. Set's associates then changed themselves into the forms of animals, and birds, and fish, but they were caught, and their heads were cut off; Set, however, who was concealed in the form of a pig, contrived to escape. The sacrifice consisted of a bull (or cow) or two, two gazelles or antelopes, and ducks. When the bull had been slain, one of the forelegs was cut off, and the heart taken out, and offered to the statue or mummy; the *Sem* priest then took the bleeding leg and touched, or pretended to touch, the mouth and eyes with it four times. The slaughtered gazelles or antelopes and ducks were simply offered before the statue. The *Sem* priest next said to the statue, "I have come to embrace thee, I am thy son Horus, I have pressed thy mouth; I am thy son, I love thee…. Thy mouth was closed, but I have set in order for thee thy mouth and thy teeth." He then brought two instruments, called "Seb-ur" and "Tuntet" respectively, and touched the mouth of the statue or mummy with them, whilst the Kher-heb said, "Thy mouth was closed, but I have set in order for thee thy mouth and thy teeth. I open for thee thy mouth, I open for thee thy two eyes. I have opened for thee thy mouth with the instrument of Anubis. I have opened thy mouth with the instrument of Anubis, with the iron implement with which the mouths of the gods were opened. Horus, open the mouth! Horus, open the mouth! Horus hath opened the mouth of the dead, as he in times of old opened the mouth of Osiris, with the iron which came forth from Set, with the iron instrument with which he opened the mouths of the gods. He hath opened thy mouth with it. The deceased shall walk and shall speak, and his body shall be with the great company of the gods in the Great House of the Aged One in Annu, and he shall receive there the *ureret* crown from Horus, the lord of mankind." Thus the mouth and the eyes of the deceased are opened. The *Sem* priest then took in his hand the instrument called *ur hekau, i.e.,* the "mighty one of enchantments," a curious, sinuous piece of wood, one end of which is in the form of a ram's head surmounted by a uraeus, and touched the mouth and the, eyes of the statue or mummy four times, whilst the *Kher-heb* recited a long address in which he declared that this portion of the ceremony had secured for the deceased all the benefits which accrued to the god Osiris from the actions of Nut, Horus, and Set, when he was in a similar state. It has been said above that every dead man hoped to be provided with the hekau, or words of power, which were necessary for him in the next world, but without a mouth it was impossible for him to utter them. Now that the mouth, or rather the use of it, was restored to the deceased, it was all important to give him not only the words of power, but also the ability to utter them correctly and in such wise that the gods and other beings would hearken to them and obey them; four touches of the *ur hekau* instrument on the lips endowed the deceased with the faculty of uttering the proper words in the proper manner in each of the four quarters of the world. When this had been done, several other ceremonies were performed with the object of allowing the "son who loveth him" or his representative to take part in the opening of the mouth of his father. In order to do this he took in his hand a metal chisel and touched the openings of the mouth and of the eyes, and then the *Sem* priest touched them first with his little finger, and afterwards with a little bag filled with pieces of red stone or carnelian, with the idea, M. Maspero thinks, of restoring to the lips and eyelids the colour which they had lost during the process of mummification. The "son who loves him" then took four objects called "iron of the South, and iron of the North," and laid each of them four times upon the mouth and the eyes while the Kher-heb recited the proper address in which the mummy or statue is said to have had his mouth and lips established firmly. This done, the *Sem* priest brings an instrument called the "Pesh-en-kef," and touches the mouth of the mummy or statue therewith, and says, "O Osiris, I have stablished for thee

the two jaw-bones in thy face, and they are now separated";
that is to say, the bandages with which they have been tied
up can no longer prevent their movement when the deceased
wishes to eat. After the Pesh-en-kef had been used the *Sem*
priest brought forward a basket or vessel of some kind of
food in the shape of balls, and by the order of the *Kher-heb*
offered them to the mouth of the mummy, and when this
portion of the ceremony was ended, the *Sem* priest took an
ostrich feather, and waved it before its face four times, but
with what object is not clear. Such are the ceremonies
which it was thought necessary to perform in order to
restore to the deceased the functions which his body
possessed upon earth. But it must be remembered that
hitherto only the "bull of the south" has been sacrificed,
and that the "bull of the north" has yet to be offered up;
and all the ceremonies which have been already performed
must be repeated if the deceased would have the power to
go forth at will over the whole earth. From the earliest
times the South and the North were the two great sections
into which the world was divided, and each section
possessed its own special gods, all of whom had to be
propitiated by the deceased; hence most religious ceremonies
were ordered to be performed in duplicate. In later days
each section was divided into two parts, and the four
divisions thus made were apportioned to the four children

of Horus; hence prayers and formulae were usually said four times, once in honour of each god, and the rubrical directions on this point are definite.

In the limited space of this book it is not possible to reproduce all the scenes of the ceremony of opening the mouth and the eyes which are depicted in the tombs and elsewhere, but this is a general view of the ceremony as it is often given in the papyri of the XVIIIth and XIXth dynasties. On the right we see the pyramidal tomb in the Theban hill with its open door, and by the side of it is the funeral stele with a rounded top inscribed with a figure of the deceased standing in adoration before Osiris, and with a prayer to the god for sepulchral offerings. Anubis, the god of the dead, embraces the mummy, thus indicating his readiness to take the deceased under his protection. Nasha, the wife of the deceased, stands weeping before the mummy, and at his feet kneels another weeping woman, probably his daughter. Anubis and the mummy stand upon a layer of sand which has been placed there with the object of sanctifying the ground. A priest clad in a panther's skin holds a censer containing burning incense in one hand, and a vase, from which he sprinkles water, in the other. One ministrant holds the two instruments "Tun-tet" and "Seb-ur" in the right hand, and the "Ur hekau" instrument in the left; and another offers four vases of unguent. In the lower register are a cow and her calf, and two men are carrying along to the mummy the haunch which we must assume to have been recently cut from the slaughtered bull, and the heart which has just been taken out of him. On a table we see lying a number of objects, the "Meskhet," and Pesh-en-kef," and other instruments, two sets of four vases for holding unguents and oil, the bags of colour, the iron of the south and north, etc. The text which runs in short vertical lines above the scene reads: "The Chapter of the opening of the mouth of the statue of Osiris, the royal scribe, Hunefer, which is to be performed [when] its face [looketh] towards the south, [and when it is set] upon the sand behind him. And the *Kher-heb* shall say four times unto the *Sem* priest as he goeth round about him bearing four vases of water: 'Thou art pure with the purification of Horus, and Horus is pure with thy purification. Thou art pure with the purification of Thoth, and Thoth is pure with thy purification. Thou art pure with the purification of Sep, and Sep is pure with thy purification. Thou art pure with the purification of Seb, and Seb is pure with thy purification. Pure. Pure.' [Say] four times. 'Incense hath been offered unto thee of the incense of Horus, and incense hath been offered unto Horus of thy incense. Incense hath been offered unto thee of the incense of Thoth, and incense hath been offered unto Thoth of thy incense. Incense hath been offered unto thee of the incense of Sep, and incense hath been offered unto Sep of thy incense. Incense hath been offered unto thee of the incense of Seb, and incense hath been offered unto Seb of thy incense.'" The above words are all the text that the scribe considered it necessary to give in the Papyrus of Hunefer, and that he curtailed the representation of the ceremony of opening the mouth and eyes as much as possible is evident.

The performance of the ceremony of opening the mouth was followed by a number of other less important ceremonies which had for their object the providing of the mummy or statue with scents, and unguents, and various articles of wearing apparel; these were not essentials, but sufficient importance was attached to them to make the performance of them almost obligatory. Among the objects presented to the deceased in these ceremonies scents and perfumed unguents play a prominent part, and this is not to be wondered at. To certain kinds of oil, magical properties have been attached from time immemorial in the East, and the important place which they occupied in the ceremonies and rituals of many nations proves that remarkable effects were expected to follow their use. The living made use of oil to soften the skin and to preserve it from the parching heat of the sun, and the dead were anointed with it during the process of mummification so that their skins might, through the magical words which were pronounced whilst it was being rubbed on them, remain soft for all time, and so that the curative properties of the oil might heal the wounds which the mummifiers had made. A glance at the medical papyri of Egypt will shew that oil appears in scores of prescriptions, and it was no less useful to the magician than to the physician in producing good or evil results. It seems to have been used with the idea of effecting transformations by the former, just as it was employed by the priest in the performance of certain important religious ceremonies, and a curious survival of this use is mentioned by Lucian, who relates that a woman transformed herself into a night-raven by its means. The woman first undressed herself, and going to a lamp threw two grains of incense into the flame and recited certain words; she then went to a large chest containing several bottles, and taking out one which, the writer thinks, contained oil, rubbed all her body with the liquid, from head to foot, beginning with the ends of the nails, and suddenly feathers and wings began to grow upon her, and a hooked, horny beak took the place of her nose. In a very short time she resembled a bird in every respect, and when she saw that she was well feathered, she flew upwards and, uttering the cry of a night-raven, disappeared through the window. In connexion with the recital of certain Chapters of the Book of the Dead a number of interesting ceremonies were performed, but as they only illustrate the beliefs described above they need not be mentioned here.

CHAPTER VII

DEMONIACAL POSSESSION, DREAMS, GHOSTS, LUCKY AND UNLUCKY DAYS, HOROSCOPES, PROGNOSTICATIONS, TRANSFORMATIONS, AND THE WORSHIP OF ANIMALS

THE Egyptians, in common with many other Eastern nations, believed that certain sicknesses and diseases might be cured by certain medicaments pure and simple, but that others needed not only drugs but the recital of words of power to effect their cure. There is good reason for thinking that some diseases were attributed to the action of evil spirits or demons, which had the power of entering into human bodies and of vexing them in proportion to their malignant nature and influence, but the texts do not afford much information on the matter. Incidentally, however, we have one interesting proof that foreign peoples believed that the Egyptians were able to cure the diseases caused by demoniacal possession, and the exercise of their power on the occasion described was considered to be so noteworthy that the narrative of it was inscribed upon a stele and setup in the temple of the god Khonsu at Thebes, so that all men might read and know what a marvellous cure his priests had effected. It appears that king Rameses II. was in Mesopotamia "according to his wont, year by year," and all the chiefs of the countries round about came to pay their respects to him, and they sought to obtain his goodwill and protection, probably even an alliance, by bringing to him gifts of gold, and lapis lazuli, and turquoise, and of every kind of valuable thing which the land produced, and every man sought to outdo his neighbour by the lavishness of his gifts. Among others there came the Prince of Bekhten, and at the head of all the offerings which he presented to His Majesty he placed his eldest daughter, who was very beautiful. When the king saw her he thought her the most beautiful girl he had ever seen, and he bestowed upon her the title of "Royal spouse, chief lady, Râ-neferu" (i.e., "the beauties of Râ," the Sun-god), and took her to Egypt; and when they arrived in that country the king married her. One day during the fifteenth year of the king's reign, when His Majesty was in Thebes celebrating the festival of Amen-Râ, a messenger came to the king and reported the arrival of an ambassador from the Prince of Bekhten who had brought rich gifts for the royal lady Râ-neferu. When he had been led into the king's presence, he did homage before him, saying, "Glory and praise be unto thee, O thou Sun of the nations; grant that we may live before thee!" Having said these words he bowed down and touched the ground with his head three times, and said, "I have come unto thee, O my sovereign Lord, on behalf of the lady Bent-ent-resht, the younger sister of the royal spouse Râ-neferu, for, behold, an evil disease hath laid hold upon her body; I beseech thy Majesty to send a physician to see her." Then the king straightway ordered the books of the "double house of life" to be brought and the learned men to appear, and when they had come into his presence he ordered them to choose from among their number a man "wise of heart and cunning of finger," that he might send him to Bekhten; they did so, and their choice fell upon one Tehuti-em-heb. This sage having come before the king was ordered to set out for Bekhten in company with the ambassador, and he departed; and when they had arrived there the Egyptian priest found the lady Bent-ent-resht to be possessed of a demon or spirit over which he was powerless. The Prince of Bekhten, seeing that the priest was unable to afford relief to his daughter, sent once again to the king, and entreated him to send a god to his help.

When the ambassador from Bekhten arrived in Egypt the king was in Thebes, and on hearing what was asked he went into the temple of Khonsu Nefer-hetep, and besought that god to allow his counterpart Khonsu to depart to Bekhten and to deliver the daughter of the prince of that country from the power of the demon that possessed her. It seems as if the sage Tehuti-em-heb had been sent to Bekhten by the advice of the god, for the king says, in addressing, the god, "I have come once again into thy presence"; but in any case Khonsu Nefer-hetep agreed to his request, and a fourfold measure of magical power was imparted to the statue of the god which was to go to Bekhten. The god, seated in his boat, and five other boats with figures of gods in them, accompanied by chariots and horses on the right hand and on the left, set out from Egypt, and after travelling for seventeen months arrived in Bekhten, where they were received with great honour. The god Khonsu went to the place where Bent-ent-resht was, and, having performed a magical ceremony over her, the demon departed from her and she was cured straightway. Then the demon addressed the Egyptian god, saying, "Grateful and welcome is thy coming unto us, O great god, thou vanquisher of the hosts of darkness! Bekhten is thy city, the inhabitants thereof are thy slaves, and I am thy servant; and I will depart unto the place whence I came that I may gratify thee, for unto this end hast thou come thither. And I beseech thy Majesty to command that the Prince of Bekhten and I may hold a festival together." To the demon's request Khonsu agreed, and he commanded his priest to tell the Prince of Bekhten to make a great festival in honour of the demon; this having been done by the command of Khonsu the demon departed to his own place.

When the Prince of Bekhten saw that Khonsu was thus powerful, he and all his people rejoiced exceedingly, and he determined that the god should not be allowed to return to Egypt, and as a result Khonsu remained in Bekhten for three years, four months, and five days. On a certain day, however, the Prince was sleeping and he dreamed a dream in which he saw the god Khonsu come forth from his shrine in the form of a hawk of gold, and having mounted into the air he flew away to Egypt. The Prince woke up in a state of great perturbation, and having inquired of the Egyptian priest was told by him that the god had departed to Egypt, and that his chariot must now be sent back. Then the Prince gave to Khonsu great gifts, and they were taken to Egypt and laid before the god Khonsu Nefer-hetep in his temple at Thebes. In early Christian literatures we find a number of examples of demoniacal possession in which the demon who has entered the body yields it up before a demon of greater power than himself, but the demon who is expelled is invariably hostile to him that expels him, and he departs from before him with every sign of wrath and shame. The fact that it was believed possible for the demon of Bekhten and the god Khonsu to fraternize, and to be present together at a festival made by the Prince of the country, shews that the people of Bekhten ascribed the same attributes to spirits or demons as they did to men. The demon who possessed the princess recognized in Khonsu a being who was mightier than himself, and, like a vanquished king, he wished to make the best terms he could with his conqueror, and to be on good terms with him.

The Egyptians believed that the divine powers frequently made known their will to them by means of dreams, and they attached considerable importance to them; the figures of the gods and the scenes which they saw when dreaming seemed to them to prove the existence of another world which was not greatly unlike that already known to them. The knowledge of the art of procuring dreams and the skill to interpret them were greatly prized in Egypt as elsewhere in the East, and the priest or official who possessed such gifts sometimes rose to places of high honour in the state, as we may see from the example of Joseph, for it was universally believed that glimpses of the future were revealed to man in dreams. As instances of dreams recorded in the Egyptian texts may be quoted those of Thothmes IV., king of Egypt about B.C. 1450, and Nut-Amen, king of the Eastern Sûdân and Egypt, about B.C. 670. A prince, according to the stele which he set up before the breast of the Sphinx at Gizeh, was one day hunting near this emblem of Râ-Harmachis, and he sat down to rest under its shadow and fell asleep and dreamed a dream. In it the god appeared to him, and, having declared that he was the god Harmachis-Khepera-Râ-Temu, promised him that if he would clear away from the Sphinx, his own image, the drift sand in which it was becoming buried, he would give to him the sovereignty of the lands of the South and of the North, *i.e.*, of all Egypt. In due course the prince became king of Egypt under the title of Thothmes IV., and the stele which is dated on the 19th day of the month Hathor of the first year of Thothmes IV. proves that the royal dreamer carried out the wishes of the god. Of Nut-Amen, the successor of the great Piânkhi who came down from Gebel Barkal and conquered all Egypt from Syene to the sea, we read that in the first year of his reign he one night dreamed a dream wherein he saw two serpents, one on his right hand and the other on his left; when he awoke they had disappeared. Having asked for an interpretation of the dream he was told:- "The land of the

South is thine, and thou shalt have dominion over the land of the North: the White Crown and the Red Crown shall adorn thy head. The length and the breadth of the land shall be given unto thee, and the god Amen, the only god, shall be with thee." The two serpents were the symbols of the goddesses Nekhebet and Uatchet, the mistresses of the South and North respectively. As the result of his dream Nut-Amen invaded Egypt successfully and brought back much spoil, a portion of which he dedicated to the service of his god Amen.

Since dreams and visions in which the future might be revealed to the sleeper were greatly desired, the Egyptian magician set himself to procure such for his clients by various devices, such as drawing magical pictures and reciting magical words. The following are examples of spells for procuring a vision and dreams, taken from British Museum Papyrus, No. 122, lines 64 ff. and 359 ff. "To obtain a vision from [the god] Bes. Make a drawing of Besa, as shewn below, on your left hand, and envelope your hand in a strip of black cloth that has been consecrated to Isis (?) and lie down to sleep without speaking a word, even in answer to a question. Wind the remainder of the cloth round your neck. The ink with which you write must be composed of the blood of a cow, the blood of a white dove, fresh (?) frankincense, myrrh, black writing-ink, cinnabar, mulberry juice, rain-water, and the juice of wormwood and vetch. With this write your petition before the setting sun, [saying], "Send the truthful seer out of the holy shrine, I beseech thee, Lampsuer, Sumarta, Baribas, Dardalam, Iorlex: O Lord send the sacred deity Anuth, Anuth, Salbana, Chambré, Breïth, now, now, quickly, quickly. Come in this very night."

"To procure dreams: Take a clean linen bag and write upon it the names given below. Fold it up and make it into a lamp-wick, and set it alight, pouring pure oil over it. The word to be written is this: 'Armiuth, Lailamchoüch, Arsenophrephren, Phtha, Archentechtha.' Then in the evening, when you are going to bed, which you must do without touching food [or, pure from all defilement], do thus. Approach the lamp and repeat seven times the formula given below: then extinguish it and lie down to sleep. The formula is this: 'Sachmu … epaëma Ligotereënch: the Aeon, the Thunderer, Thou that hast swallowed the snake and dost exhaust the moon, and dost raise up the orb of the sun in his season, Chthetho is thy name; I require, O lords of the gods, Seth, Chreps, give me the information that I desire.'"

The peculiar ideas which the Egyptians held about the composition of man greatly favoured the belief in apparitions and ghosts. According to them a man consisted of a physical body, a shadow, a double, a soul, a heart, a spirit called the *khu*, a power, a name, and a spiritual body. When the body died the shadow departed from it, and could only be brought back to it by the performance of a mystical ceremony; the double lived in the tomb with the body, and was there visited by the soul whose habitation was in heaven. The soul was, from one aspect, a material thing, and like the *ka*, or double, was believed to partake of the funeral offerings which were brought to the tomb; one of the chief objects of sepulchral offerings of meat and drink was to keep the double in the tomb and to do away with the necessity of its wandering about outside the tomb in search of food. It is clear from many texts that, unless the double was supplied with sufficient food, it would wander forth from the tomb and eat any kind of offal and drink any kind of dirty water which it might find in its path. But besides the shadow, and the double, and the soul, the spirit of the deceased, which usually had its abode in heaven, was sometimes to be found in the tomb. There is, however, good reason for stating that the immortal part of man which lived in the tomb and had its special abode in the statue of the deceased was the "double." This is proved by the fact that a special part of the tomb was reserved for the *ka*, or double, which was called the "house of the *ka*," and that a priest, called the "priest of the *ka*," was specially appointed to minister therein. The double enjoyed the smell of the incense which was offered at certain times each year in the tomb, as well as the flowers, and herbs, and meat, and drink; and the statue of the deceased in which the double dwelt took pleasure in all the various scenes which were painted or sculptured on the walls of the various chambers of the tomb, and enjoyed again all the delights which his body had enjoyed upon earth. The *ka*, or double, then, in very early times was, to all intents and purposes, the ghost of the Egyptians. In later times the *khu*, or "spirit," seems to have been identified with it, and there are frequent allusions in the texts to the sanctity of the offerings made to the *khu*, and to their territories, *i.e.*, the districts in which their mummified bodies lie.

Whether there was any general belief that the *ka* or *khu* could or did hold intercourse with his relatives or friends whom he left alive upon earth cannot be said, but an instance is known in which a husband complains to his wife, who has been dead for three years, of the troubles which she has brought upon him since her death. He describes his own merits and the good treatment which he had vouchsafed to her when she was alive, and declares that the evil with which she is requiting him is not to be endured. To make his complaint to reach her he first reduced it to writing upon papyrus, then went to her tomb and read it there, and finally tied the papyrus to a statue or figure of his wife which was therein; since her double or spirit lived in the tomb she would, of course, read the writing and understand it. It is a pity that we have no means of knowing what was the result of the husband's complaint. Elsewhere we have a fragment of a conversation which a priest of Amen called Khonsu-em-heb, who was searching for a suitable place in which to build his tomb, holds with the double or spirit of some person whom he has disturbed, and the spirit of the dead tells some details of his life to the living man. The cemeteries were regarded with awe by the ancient Egyptians because of the spirits of the dead who dwelt in them, and even the Arabic-speaking peoples of Egypt and the Sûdân, if we exclude the "antiquity grubber," have them in great respect for the same reason. The modern peoples of the Sûdân firmly believe that the spirits of those slain in battle dwell on the field where they fell, or where their bodies are buried, and the soldiers in the tenth battalion of Lord Kitchener's army declare that the grave of the gallant Major Sidney, who was shot while charging at the head of his regiment, in the battle of Abû Hamed, August 7th, 1897, "is watched regularly every night by the ghosts of the native soldiers who were killed at Abû Hamed, and who mount guard over their dead commander's tomb, challenging, with every military detail, all passers-by. So implicitly is this legend credited by the blacks that none of them will, after dusk, approach the grave. Any one doing so is believed to be promptly halted by a phantom sentry, and even the words (in Arabic), 'Guard, turn out!' are often (so the story goes) plainly heard repeated at some distance off across the desert."

The Egyptians believed that a man's fate or destiny was decided before he was born, and that he had no power whatever to alter it. Their sages, however, professed to be able to declare what the fate might be, provided that they were given certain data, that is to say, if they were told the date of his birth, and if they were able to ascertain the position of the planets and stars at that time. The goddess of fate or destiny was called "Shai," and she is usually accompanied by another goddess called "Renenet," who is commonly regarded as the lady of fortune; they both appear in the Judgment Scene, where they seem to watch the weighing of the heart on behalf of the deceased. But another goddess, Meskhenet, is sometimes present, and she also seems to have had influence over a man's future; in any case she was able to predict what that future was to be. Thus we read that she and Isis, and Nephthys, and Heqet, disguised as women, went to the house of Râ-user, whose wife Râ-Tettet was in travail; when they had been taken into her room they assisted her in giving birth to triplets, and as each child was born Meskhenet declared, "He shall be a king who shall have dominion over the whole land." And this prophecy was fulfilled, for the three boys became three of the kings of the Vth dynasty. The Seven Hathor goddesses also could predict the future of a human being, for in the well-known "Tale of Two Brothers" it is related that, when the god Khnemu, at the request of Râ-Harmachis, had created for Bata a wife "who was more beautiful in her person than any other woman in all the earth, for the essence of every god was contained in her," they came to see her, and that they spake with one voice, saying, "Her death will be caused by the knife." And this came to pass, for, according to the story, when the king whose wife she became heard from her first husband that she had left him and had wrought evil against him, he entered into judgment with her in the presence of his chiefs and nobles, and "one carried out their decree," *i.e.*, they sentenced her to death and she was executed. Similarly, in another story, the Seven Hathors came to see the son who had been born to a certain king in answer to his prayers to the gods, and when they had seen him they said, "He shall die by means of a crocodile, or a serpent, or a dog." The story goes on to say how he escaped from the crocodile and the serpent, and though the end is wanting, it is quite clear that he was wounded by an accidental bite of his dog and so died. The moral of all such stories is that there is no possibility of avoiding fate, and it is most probable that the modern Egyptian has only inherited his ancestors' views as to its immutability. A man's life might, however, be happy or unhappy according as the hour of the day or the day itself was lucky or unlucky, and every day of the Egyptian year was divided into three parts, each of which was lucky or unlucky. When Olympias was about to give birth to Alexander the Great, Nectanebus stood by her making observations of the heavenly bodies, and from time to time he besought her to restrain herself until the auspicious hour had arrived; and it was not until he saw a certain splendour in the sky and knew that all the heavenly bodies were in a favourable position that he permitted her to bring forth her child. And when he had said, "O queen, now thou wilt give birth to a governor of the world," the child fell upon the ground while the earth quaked, and the lightnings flashed, and the thunder roared. Thus it is quite evident that the future of a child depended even upon the hour in which he was born.

In magical papyri we are often told not to perform certain magical ceremonies on such and such days, the idea being that on these days hostile powers will make them to be powerless, and that gods mightier than those to which the petitioner would appeal will be in the ascendant. There have come down to us, fortunately, papyri containing copies of the Egyptian calendar, in which each third of every day for three hundred and sixty days of the year is marked lucky or unlucky, and we know from other papyri why certain days were lucky or unlucky, and why others were only partly so. Taking the month Thoth, which was the first month of the Egyptian year, and began, according to the Gregorian Calendar, on August 29th, we find that the days are marked as follows:-

Now the sign ⚑ means "lucky," and ⚑ means "unlucky"; thus at a glance it could be seen which third of the day is lucky or unlucky, and the man who consulted the calendar would, of course, act accordingly. It must be noted that the priests or magicians who drew up the calendar had good reasons for their classification of the days, as we may see from the following example. The 19th day of Thoth is, in the above list, marked wholly lucky, *i.e.*, each third of it is lucky, and the papyrus Sallier IV. also marks it wholly lucky, and adds the reason:- "It is a day of festival in heaven and upon earth in the presence of Râ. It is the day when flame was hurled upon those who followed the boat containing the shrine of the gods; and on this day the gods gave praises being content," etc. But in both lists the 26th day is marked wholly unlucky, the reason being, "This was the day of the fight between Horus and Set." They first fought in the form of men, then they took the form of bears, and in this state did battle with each other for three days and three nights. Isis aided Set when he was getting the worst in the fight, and Horus thereupon cut off his mother's head, which Thoth transformed by his words of power into that of a cow and put on her body. On this day offerings are to be made to Osiris and Thoth, but work of any kind is absolutely forbidden. The calendars of lucky and unlucky days do not, however, always agree as to a given day. Thus in the list given above the 20th day of Thoth is marked wholly unlucky, but in the papyrus Sallier IV. it is wholly lucky, but the reader is told not to do any work in it, nor to slay oxen, nor to receive a stranger; on this day the gods who are in the following of Râ slew the rebels. Concerning the fourth day of the next month, Paophi, the papyrus Sallier IV. says, "Go not forth from thy house from any side of it; whosoever is born on this day shall die of the disease *aat*." Concerning the fifth day it says, "Go not forth from thy house from any side of it, and hold no intercourse with women. This is the day wherein all things were performed in the divine presence, and the majesty of the god Menthu was satisfied therein. Whosoever is born on this day shall die of excessive venery." Concerning the ninth day it says, "Whosoever is born on this day shall die of old age," and concerning the fifteenth, "Go not forth from thy dwelling at eventide, for the serpent Uatch, the son of the god, goeth forth at this time, and misfortunes follow him; whosoever shall see him shall lose his eye straightway."

Again, the twenty-sixth day of Paophi was a lucky day for making the plan of a house; on the fifth day of Hathor no fire was to be kindled in the house; on the sixteenth day it was forbidden to listen to songs of joy because on this day Isis and Nephthys wept for Osiris at Abydos; a man born on the twenty-third day would die by drowning; and so on. But to the three hundred and sixty days given in the calendars of lucky and unlucky days must be added the five epagomenal days which were considered to be of great importance and had each its peculiar name. On the first Osiris was born, on the second Heru-ur (Aroueris), on the third Set, on the fourth Isis, and on the fifth Nephthys; the first, third, and fifth of these days were unlucky, and no work of any kind was to be undertaken on them. The rubric which refers to these days states that whosoever knoweth their names shall never suffer from thirst, that he shall never be smitten down by disease, and that the goddess Sekhet shall never take possession of him; it also directs that figures of the five gods mentioned above shall be drawn with unguent and *ânti* scent upon a piece of fine linen, evidently to serve as an amulet.

From the life of Alexander the Great by Pseudo-Callisthenes we learn that the Egyptians were skilled in the art of casting nativities, and that knowing the exact moment of the birth of a man they proceeded to construct his horoscope. Nectanebus employed for the purpose a tablet made of gold and silver and acacia wood, to which were fitted three belts. Upon the outer belt was Zeus with the thirty-six *decani* surrounding him; upon the second the twelve signs of the Zodiac were represented; and upon the third the sun and moon. He set the tablet upon a tripod, and then emptied out of a small box upon it models of the seven stars that were in the belts, and put into the middle belt eight precious stones; these he arranged in the places wherein he supposed the planets which they represented would be at the time of the birth of Olympias, and then told her fortune from them. But the use of the horoscope is much older than the time of Alexander the Great, for to a Greek horoscope in the British Museum is attached "an introductory letter from some master of the art of astrology to his pupil, named Hermon, urging him to be very exact and careful in his application of the laws which he ancient Egyptians, with their laborious devotion to the art, had discovered and handed down to posterity." Thus we have good reason for assigning the birthplace of the horoscope to Egypt. In connexion with the horoscope must be mentioned the "sphere" or "table" of Democritus (see page 230) as a means of making predictions as to life and death. In a magical papyrus we are told to "ascertain in what month the sick man took to his bed, and the name he received at his birth. Calculate the [course of] the moon, and see how many periods of thirty days have elapsed; then note in the table the number of days left over, and if the number comes in the upper part of the table, he will live, but if in the lower part, he will die."

Both from the religious and profane literature of Egypt we learn that the gods and man in the future life were able at will to assume the form of any animal, or bird, or plant, or living thing, which they pleased, and one of the greatest delights to which a man looked forward was the possession of that power. This is proved by the fact that no less than twelve of the chapters of the Book of the Dead are devoted to providing the deceased with the words of power, the recital of which was necessary to enable him to transform himself into a "hawk of gold," a "divine hawk," "the governor of the sovereign princes," "the god who giveth light in the darkness," a lotus, the god Ptah, a *bennu* bird (*i.e.*, phœnix), a heron, a "living soul," a swallow, the serpent Sata, and a crocodile; and another chapter enabled him to transform himself into "whatever form he pleaseth." Armed with this power he could live in the water in the form of a crocodile, in the form of a serpent he could glide over the rocks and ground, in the form of the birds mentioned above he could fly through the air, and soar up and perch himself upon the bow of the boat of Râ, in the form of the lotus he had mastery over the plants of the field, and in the form of Ptah he became "more powerful than the lord of time, and shall gain the mastery over millions of years." The *bennu* bird, it will be remembered, was said to be the "soul of Râ," and

1	10	19
2	11	20
3	13	23
4	14	25
7	16	26
9	17	27
5	15	22
6	18	28
8	21	29
12	24	30

The Table of Democritus

by assuming this form the deceased identified himself with Khepera, the great god of creation, and thus acquired the attributes of the soul of the Sun-god. In the Elysian Fields he was able to assume any form and to swim and fly to any distance in any direction. It is noteworthy that no beast of the field or wild animal is mentioned as a type of his possible transformations into animals.

Now the Egyptians believed that as the souls of the departed could assume the form of any living thing or plant, so the "gods," who in many respects closely resembled them, could and did take upon themselves the forms of birds and beasts; this was the fundamental idea of the so-called "Egyptian animal worship," which provoked the merriment of the cultured Greek, and drew down upon the Egyptians the ridicule and abuse of the early Christian writers. But if the matter be examined closely its apparent stupidity disappears. The Egyptians paid honour to certain birds, and animals, and reptiles, because they considered that they possessed certain of the characteristics of the gods to whom they made them sacred. The bull was a type of the strength and procreative power of the god of reproduction in nature, and the cow was the type of his female counterpart; every sacred animal and living thing possessed some quality or attribute which was ascribed to some god, and as each god was only a form of Râ, the quality or attribute ascribed to him was that of the Sun-god himself. The educated Egyptian never worshipped an animal as an animal, but only as an incarnation of a god, and the reverence paid to animals in Egypt was in no way different from that paid to the king, who was regarded as "divine" and as an incarnation of Râ the Sun-god, who was the visible symbol of the Creator. The relation of the king to Râ was identical with that of Râ to God. The Hebrews, Greeks, and Romans never understood the logical conception which underlay the reverence with which the Egyptians regarded certain animals, and as a result they grossly misrepresented their religion. The ignorant people, no doubt, often mistook the symbol for what it symbolized, but it is wrong to say that the Egyptians worshipped animals in the ordinary sense of the word, and this fact cannot be too strongly insisted on. Holding the views he did about transformations there was nothing absurd in the reverence which the Egyptian paid to animals. When a sacred animal died the god whom it represented sought out another animal of the same species in which to renew his incarnation, and the dead body of the animal, inasmuch as it had once been the dwelling-place of a god, was mummified and treated in much the same way as a human body after death, in order that it might enjoy immortality. These views seem strange, no doubt, to us when judged by modern ideas, but they formed an integral part of the religious beliefs of the Egyptians, from the earliest to the latest times. What is remarkable, however, is the fact that, in spite of invasions, and foreign wars, and internal dissensions, and external influences of all kinds, the Egyptians clung to their gods and the sometimes childish and illogical methods which they adopted in serving them with a conservatism and zeal which have earned for them the reputation of being at once the most religious and most superstitious nation of antiquity. Whatever literary treasures may be brought to light in the future as the result of excavations in Egypt, it is most improbable that we shall ever receive from that country any ancient Egyptian work which can properly be classed among the literature of atheism or freethought; the

Egyptian might be more or less religious according to his nature and temperament, but, judging, from the writings of his priests and teachers which are now in our hands, the man who was without religion and God in some form or other was most rare, if not unknown.

INDEX